CHANGE A
LETTER,
CHANGE YOUR
LIFE

D. L. KLINE

BALBOA.
PRESS

A DIVISION OF HAY HOUSE

This book is a work of non-fiction. Unless otherwise noted, the author and the publisher make no explicit guarantees as to the accuracy of the information contained in this book and in some cases, names of people and places have been altered to protect their privacy.

Balboa Press books may be ordered through booksellers or by contacting:

Balboa Press
A Division of Hay House
1663 Liberty Drive
Bloomington, IN 47403
www.balboapress.com
1 (877) 407-4847

Because of the dynamic nature of the Internet, any web addresses or links contained in this book may have changed since publication and may no longer be valid. The views expressed in this work are solely those of the author and do not necessarily reflect the views of the publisher, and the publisher hereby disclaims any responsibility for them.

The author of this book does not dispense medical advice or prescribe the use of any technique as a form of treatment for physical, emotional, or medical problems without the advice of a physician, either directly or indirectly. The intent of the author is only to offer information of a general nature to help you in your quest for emotional and spiritual well-being. In the event you use any of the information in this book for yourself, which is your constitutional right, the author and the publisher assume no responsibility for your actions.

Any people depicted in stock imagery provided by Getty Images are models, and such images are being used for illustrative purposes only. Certain stock imagery © Getty Images.

Print information available on the last page.

ISBN: 978-1-9822-0009-1 (sc)
ISBN: 978-1-9822-0011-4 (hc)
ISBN: 978-1-9822-0010-7 (e)

Library of Congress Control Number: 2018902948

Balboa Press rev. date: 05/08/2018

Contents

Also by D. L. Kline

Suddenly Psychic

Clearing the Track

The College of Spiritual Knowledge

A Matter of Death and Life

To Pookie and the Poodle, ever and always

Preface

So, I was just sitting there, minding my own business like I always try to do, when I felt the presence of a new energy in my head.

Ever since this journey began for me a few years ago, it's been like Grand Central Station in there, with people coming and going all the time, so I wasn't really too surprised to hear from someone new.

This entity appeared as a woman dressed in a long evening gown, and she was turning boxes on a big letter board, exactly like the ever-lovely Vanna White does on Wheel of Fortune every night at seven o'clock (check your local listings).

At first, I thought it was my main spirit guide, Jasper, fooling around again.

He has a propensity for playing dress up to get my attention and illustrate whatever point he is trying to get across. He relishes making light of my puny human brain, and he has shown me that teaching me anything is like feeding a baby bird with an eyedropper, so nothing he does—or anything about his appearance—surprises me.

But this time, it wasn't Jasper in one of his many guises.

It was an entirely new spirit guide named Lorna. She said she would be helping me with the writing of this book, the concept of which is the launching of a new initiative from the other side to give those of us incarnated here on earth a better understanding of one of the basic governing principles of the universe, the law of attraction.

All of our friends at home, or on the other side, whichever you prefer, are constantly trying to help us in our earth lives by sending us messages about the nature of how the universe functions.

One of the most basic principles that they are attempting to tell us about at this time is the aforementioned law of attraction.

Entire books have been written about it, and many authors have tried in many different ways to explain how it functions and affects our lives, but to put it simply, the law of attraction says that you get back whatever you put out there.

In the vernacular of organized religion, it would be: "Do unto others as you would have them do unto you." In more secular language, it would be: "Like attracts like."

Any way you choose to think about it, it boils down to this: If you put out a lot of negativity, then that is what comes back to you, and if you put out positive energy, then positive energy will come back to you.

Now you're probably asking, if all this knowledge and information is so well known and well established that it has become a universal law, what would be the purpose of the other side launching a new initiative to rehash it?

The answer is that when we are here on earth, we choose to ignore much of the information the other side tries to give us through our spirit guides, and we have that pesky amnesia that won't let us remember most of what we know about our lives at home.

For those reasons, they keep telling us things in as many ways as possible, hoping that something will cause that light bulb moment in more and more people.

That brings us to *Change a Letter, Change Your Life.*

What better way to reintroduce and repackage an old idea than to use America's favorite game show?

Jasper, as those of you who have read my other books already know, loves him some show business. He is all about using the letter board to tell us that we can win a big prize by changing one letter in a simple, five-word phrase. The prize is not a new car or a pair of ceramic Dalmatians; it is a new outlook on life.

And what, I hear you asking, is that magical phrase?

It's one that we've all used time and again, and it often colors the way we view our life scenarios.

Without further ado, that phrase is: I believe when I see. Is there anyone out there who hasn't uttered those words or similar ones at some time in their lives? Anybody? Bueller? Bueller? I didn't think so.

Your sister, the Tupperware hoarder, is going to return your deviled egg carrier? You'll believe it when you see it. Your deadbeat cousin is going to return the money he borrowed? You'll believe it when you see it. And on and on.

Well, you may say, that's just reality. That's the way of the world.

It only works like that if you believe that it has to be that way.

On a bigger scale, if you constantly think you never have enough money to even pay the bills, then you will never have enough money to pay the bills because the universe always wants to match your thoughts and give you what it thinks you want.

The law applies to individuals, countries, and the entire planet.

For example, more than forty years ago, the Nixon administration decided to declare a war on drugs. And what is the result four decades down the road? More violence and drugs than anyone ever imagined possible.

And why? Because the universe saw we, as a nation, were focused on war and drugs. It always gives us what it seems we want—so here we are.

The same is true and happening in the war on terror. We have more violence and terror attacks than ever because people are glued to the twenty-four-hour news outlets when there is yet another attack, so the universe is giving us more of what it perceives we want to see: more war and more terror.

Only by turning our attention to the root causes of these problems and trying to make improvements there are we ever going to solve them.

In our new initiative, our new way of thinking, we're going to change that *w* in *when* to a *t* so that the resulting updated phrase becomes: I believe *then* I see.

What a difference one letter can make! It can change everything from a negative and stagnant approach to life to a positive and forward-thinking stance.

Unfortunately, changing that one letter in your belief system may be one of the hardest things you ever have to do. It means giving up your old thought processes and early programming and moving fearlessly ahead into uncharted territory.

Fortunately, Lorna and the other guides are here to give us a lot of information about how to do just that.

That deviled egg carrier your sister refuses to give back? That may be a lost cause, but learning how to have enough money to pay the bills every month? I think we've got that one covered.

This book is going to delve much more deeply into all the things the other side is trying to show us to help us live more spiritual lives while incarnated, and how to use the law of attraction to our advantage.

This old dog can't wait to be taught some new tricks, so join me as we learn together.

Don't Tell Me What Kind of Day to Have

"Have a nice day."

I'm sure that phrase was around before the 1970s, but I think that decade is when it came into wide usage. It was closely linked to the smiley-face poster seen on so many dorm room walls back then.

That symbol has morphed into the many emojis of the little yellow guy smiling in a lot of different ways that are all over our text messages.

It may have also had some connection to all those hippies smoking pot and getting high back then. Purely by coincidence, I don't remember much about that time.

Wherever and whenever it originated, to some people, it has become the singularly most annoying phrase that has ever been uttered in the history of the English language.

Does this sound familiar to anyone out there? On a typical day, you get out of bed in the morning feeling grouchy, cut yourself shaving, and burn yourself on the hot water in the shower.

Then you leave the house (late), already convinced that your day is going to suck. You hate your life and everything about it. You stop somewhere for coffee, and the damn clerk has the gall to tell you to have a nice day. It's almost more than you can bear.

You probably just grumble something and walk away, but what you'd really like to say is, "Don't tell me what kind of day to have"—or maybe something a little saltier.

I think at one time or another, we've all been there, feeling so angry about anything and everything that having a nice day wouldn't be possible if we hit the lottery and won a million dollars.

Even that would make us angrier because we'd have to pay taxes on our winnings.

This was the story of a big part of my life. Always angry. Always filled with negativity. Always miserable and unhappy.

The sad part is, a lot of the time, I didn't even know why I was so angry or what I was angry about. It was a constant background noise of negativity in my life, and everything that happened that I didn't like or wasn't happy with just added to it.

I hated my job, some of my coworkers, idiot drivers on the road, stupid sales clerks who didn't have the common courtesy to say "Thank you" when I checked out at a store (actually, that one still bothers me a little), anybody or anything that I thought was wasting my time, and especially anybody or anything that I thought interfered with my plans or my timeline for how I thought things should or would happen.

Just anger in varying degrees, twenty-four seven. When I think back to carrying around all that anger, it's a wonder my head didn't actually explode at some point.

But where was it all coming from? I think with me, as well as with a lot of other people, it all had its roots in my childhood.

You get angry with your parents for any number of reasons, but expressing that anger only leads to punishment of some kind, so you learn to bottle it all up and keep it inside.

You never learned to deal with it in any positive way because you never allowed yourself to examine it and determine what was causing it. The only thing you learned was how to suppress it enough to avoid being punished for expressing your anger.

As you grew older, you developed those same feelings of suppressed anger toward your teachers, employers, and significant others—basically the world at large.

Those of us who are survivors of our children's teenage years remember the sighs and eye rolls that almost made us snap, but we usually let them get away with it because we loved them and it was illegal to kill them.

Luckily, most people learn at least some coping skills along the way; otherwise, we'd all turn into mass murderers.

But even with those skills in place, a lot of us have that anger bubbling right under the surface that can send us into a rage over some minor little thing.

I can recall more than a few times in the past when I embarrassed myself (and probably my poor wife) by losing my temper.

And how did losing my temper and making a public spectacle make me feel afterward? Certainly not any better about myself or the situation that caused my outburst. I felt stupid, guilty, and even angrier at myself for losing control. More fuel to add to that always burning bonfire of anger inside of me.

One of the best ways to think about how not controlling and dealing with your anger affects you on a daily basis is to picture yourself as a statue made of clay.

Then imagine that every time you lose your temper, you take a big handful of yourself and throw at it whoever or whatever is making you angry: a stupid driver, your jerk boss, TV news, your spouse, your kids, etc.

By the end of the day, if you are a really angry person, there will be nothing left but a skeleton—bare bones with no energy left to function as a human being.

It's a pretty graphic image, but it sends a pretty clear message.

Stop throwing away your energy in anger because you're throwing yourself and your life away with it.

As I am writing this, one of the most contentious elections ever to occur is going on. Anger is everywhere, inflaming people on both sides of the issues. Nearly everyone feels the need to take a stand, and people seem to think that if they get angry enough and say enough nasty and hurtful things, then surely everyone on the other side of the issue will see the light and convert to their positions, which is clearly the correct and true one.

But really, how's that working out for any of you? Whether it's about national politics, a dispute at work, or a disagreement among friends, family, or neighbors, are your anger and righteous indignation changing anyone's mind?

I know you may be thinking that if you become increasingly angry and obstinate, it will only be a matter of time until everybody sees that you are absolutely correct about everything, and then everybody who disagrees with you will change their minds and positions and join you for a time of hand-holding and singing "Kumbaya," right?

Wrong. If you are reading this book, then I assume you are at least thinking about your spiritual side and are coming to understand that some things in your life just don't seem right and could be made better by making some changes in the way you think about things.

If that is indeed the case, then I think you have enough insight to know that never in the history of the planet has that last scenario I described happened on any level.

In fact, in our current situation, increasing anger on the part of some doesn't bring people closer. It makes them move away faster because you never know when some whack job is going to pull out a gun and start shooting.

So, the big question becomes, How do we even begin to move ourselves away from being immersed in this culture of anger that is so pervasive in the world today? It may sound simplistic, but one of the first steps you can take—and I know this one works because I've done it myself—is to stop watching television news.

I may watch the local news to see the weather report, but no national news, and most certainly no twenty-four-hour news channels, especially the one that has a political agenda of keeping people afraid and angry all the time.

It may seem silly or stupid to not want to be immediately informed about all the latest breaking and usually bad news, but it's been shown that moving away from the twenty-four-hour news cycle has actually improved the quality of life for a lot of people.

Noted thinkers such as Andrew Weil and Deepak Chopra have recommended greatly limiting the amount of time spent watching TV.

In fact, Dr. Weil recommends not watching television at all.

But beyond that, do you really need to hear what horrendous or insulting thing has been said by one candidate about the other? Does it nourish your soul to hear in great detail about the latest atrocity committed by one group or the other in the world's war zones? Does it increase your spirituality to know about the newest ways that people have learned to treat other people badly?

I know where I live, the local news mostly consists of where and when the latest street shooting has occurred and how many people were killed or wounded. My wife and I often comment that, sad as it is, there would only be something different in the news if they could announce that there were no shootings in a twenty-four-hour period.

Does having that very specific knowledge of all that violence and terror add anything to or enhance the quality of your spiritual life in any way?

The answer has to be a resounding no.

Are we supposed to be like hermits and not be aware of anything going on in the world at large? Again, the answer is no.

We incarnate here to learn what it feels like to live in an environment of near-total negativity, and with every passing day, our learning goals are being met. The big piece of the puzzle that some of us are missing, however, is the part that lets us process all the craziness that is going on around us without letting it become the major focus of our lives.

Before I go into great detail about the new way of thinking about and dealing with all the negativity in the world that has been provided to us by our friends on the other side, let me restate something I wrote about in my last book.

In *A Matter of Death and Life,* I went on at length about the very intricate plans we make for each of our earth lives before we incarnate. That means that I have a life plan, you have a life plan, murder victims have a life plan, terrorists have a life plan, and refugees have a life plan.

For better or worse, in sickness and in health, we all have our own life plans.

Just because you or I couldn't begin to understand why some souls would plan for horrific things to happen to them or ask another soul to commit those horrific acts to aid them in their learning and soul growth, it doesn't mean it wasn't all planned out that way.

Having the knowledge and understanding that this is, indeed, the way the universe works can help you overcome the feelings of fear and anger that happen when you become heavily invested in knowing what is going on in every part of the world every hour of every day. It can help you truly know that having access to that constant flow of information does nothing to aid you in your spiritual advancement.

But I digress. Let me get back to the new way of thinking that the other side has provided us as a way of helping us move from being in a constant state of negativity, fear, and anger to a more positive way of being and an increased vibrational level.

First and foremost, you have to actually recognize that you are in a state of anger a great deal of the time. Otherwise, you won't be ready to do the spiritual work necessary to move away from that negativity and deal with it.

It might be that after a particularly nasty outburst on your part, you come to the realization that you are acting like a real jackass and start feeling remorseful. Or it might be that you just get tired of constantly thinking and feeling the worst about everybody and everything in your life.

As I previously described, there is a constant drain on your energy if you are throwing pieces of yourself away in anger.

Whatever may set you off, you have to reach a low point where you say to yourself, "This is not me, and this is not the way I want to be perceived by everyone around me." Then, and only then, can real change begin.

Start by figuring out what your triggers are and what causes your anger to reach the boiling point.

Does it happen most often when you are with family and friends or when you are at work? Is it most often when you're driving, shopping, or in some other situation with people you don't know personally?

You may find, once you actually start to make a mental list, that there are a lot of people and/or scenarios that can trigger your anger, so you've got to catalog as many as you can identify.

The general overview of the anger-management plan that the guides have provided has us go from listing all our specific negatives, learning to deal with them, and then moving on to more general negatives, dealing with them and turning them into very general positives, and finally ending up with naming and enjoying all the specific positives in our lives.

This first step in identifying our triggers is also the first step in naming the things we identify as specifically negative.

So, to use a very common example, let's say we are the nicest people around until we get behind the wheel of a car. Then, because of our inability to control our anger, we turn into raving maniacs, driving dangerously and screaming at other drivers.

We've all read and heard stories about road rage, especially when it's been taken to the extreme of someone running another driver off the road or pulling a gun and shooting someone. If this describes you, even in its mildest form, or someone you know, you have to ask why.

Why do you do it? Who does your screaming, swearing and stupid driving have the most effect on? You or the other drivers? If you're being honest with yourself, you have to know that you are hurting yourself more than anybody else.

Your blood pressure and heart rate go up, sometimes to alarming levels, and a simple drive to work can alter your mood in a negative way for the rest of the working day.

Then it's time for the drive home, and the nasty scenario can repeat itself.

Just as Dean Wormer said to Flounder in that famous scene from *Animal House*: "Fat, drunk, and stupid is no way to go through life, son." Tense, angry, and miserable is no way to go through life either.

Once you admit to yourself that there are times when you just lose control and start acting like a jerk, you can identify what is happening around you at those specific times and start to deal with the situations you are in.

Let's say you hear yourself screaming at other drivers when they don't use their turn signals or when they cut you off in traffic. This is good. Now you can name a specific action by someone else that you know can set off an angry tirade.

When confronted with that situation, you can stop and say, "Okay, here's where I usually lose it, but this time, I will not be screaming obscenities or flipping the bird. This time, I'm going to let it go and wish the other driver Godspeed as he continues his life journey."

Or you can use other words to that effect. I can hear the laughter out there, but if you truly want to learn to control your anger and move your life from being mostly negative to being mostly positive, you've got to start somewhere, so why not here?

Again, if we are going to conquer all or most of the specific negativity in our lives, eliminating something as simple and as common as road rage to whatever degree you have it is as a good a place as any to start. It's probably something you encounter almost every day, and once you deal with it, you can let it go.

You can then begin to list all the other individual and specific negative things in your life, and you can deal with them in the same way. After you get control over the first one or two scenarios, the rest should begin to fall like dominoes until all the things that are bringing negativity into your life have been dealt with.

This might be a good time to talk some more about the importance of control.

Let there be no doubt about it: we are always the ones in control of our emotions. You may think that jerk who just cut you off in traffic is the one who is making you angry, but he is not. You are making yourself angry in response to something somebody else around you did.

You could just as easily think, *So what?* As a wise old friend of mine used to say in similar situations, "Fifty years from now, who's gonna remember?"

We always have control over our emotions, but we choose not to exercise that control much of the time. It's easier to go with your gut reaction than to stop and actually think about how to respond to a given situation.

The world could be a much more peaceful place to live if we could all learn to say, "So what?" a lot more and flip the bird a lot less.

Let me be perfectly clear. I'm not advocating suppressing anger here because that can lead to a whole host of problems, especially including physical issues like ulcers, high blood pressure, and heart disease. I'm talking about an attitude of truly letting go of anger or—even better—not getting angry in the first place.

One of the bad habits we can develop, or one that we can use to displace some of our anger without getting rid of it entirely, is getting a case of the "yeah-buts."

If a "so what" attitude is what we're striving for when we start to deal with our anger issues, it's the yeah-buts that can sabotage us during the development of our new way of thinking.

A case of the yeah-buts can develop most often when dealing with friends, neighbors, family members, and coworkers. Let's use that rich pool of inspiration to give us an example.

Let's say you have one of those neighbors who is always coming over to borrow something—the wife is always in need of a cup of sugar, and the husband always needs your hedge clippers—and they never return anything.

You are forever having to go next door and ask for your sugar or your hedge clippers back, which makes you angry and leads to you swearing you will never loan them anything again.

Without a doubt, a few weeks later, they will need the sugar and/or the hedge clippers again, and of course you say okay.

The cycle begins again with any number of household products until your anger builds to the point that you blow your top and tell them to go home and never come back.

Of course, you feel guilty the next day, go next door to apologize, and tell yourself you are turning over a new leaf.

You are totally done with being angry, it serves no purpose, and you are not going to become angry anymore. Until a few days later when your neighbor comes over to borrow your hedge clippers … again. And you say okay and hand them over.

Here is where the yeah-buts begin. You say to yourself, "Yeah, I'm done being angry, but honest to god, if he doesn't return my hedge clippers this time, I will lose my freakin' mind." Sorry, but that's not the way this all works.

Either you're done being angry—or you're not. No yeah-buts. And why don't you buy yourself a new pair of hedge clippers and let him keep your old ones? It's a win-win all around.

The point of this whole discussion is to identify all the specific negativity in your life by learning to see it in yourself, recognize it as it's happening, and having the presence of mind to say, "Oh, yeah, that's what makes me angry and leads to these embarrassing outbursts."

In this age of ubiquitous cell phone cameras, ask someone who is around you a lot to video you when you are being a jerk, with the caveat that they promise not to post it on social media. This is a tool to use for learning and not for pubic shaming.

Do whatever it takes to help you gain insight into your behavior and then acknowledge and own it. Like every emotional issue we all have, you have to name it to claim it. Once you have done that, you can shut down these situations one by one and work on getting those many niggling pieces of negativity under control.

Having gained control over as many specific anger-inducing scenarios as you can, you can start to think about the more general negativity that sometimes creates the backdrop for a large portion of our lives. You might even consider it to be the *why* in why you hate your life.

It can be big things, like world events or politics, that no matter what you do, you are not going to have any real effect on, so you shouldn't let them have any real effect on you. As I discussed before, turn off your TV.

Sometimes, it is much smaller and more personal than those type of things. It may be a bad relationship or a job you really don't like. Stop, take the time to think, and figure out exactly what is making you miserable.

Borrowing from an old quote by Benjamin Franklin about beer being proof that god loves us and wants us to be happy, the universe does love us unconditionally and wants us to be happy.

This life that we incarnate here to experience is supposed to be fun and joyous—even when it isn't for varying periods of time. We are not here to suffer and be tortured as organized religion would have us believe.

Someone once wrote that the definition of a religious conservative is a person who lives in constant fear that somewhere people are actually enjoying life.

Don't fall into that role of martyrdom because it can bring all spiritual growth to a screeching halt.

But I digress. If you do a lot of soul-searching and determine that it is a relationship or a job that is bringing negativity into your life, then it's time to make a change in one or both of those areas.

None of us are here to play the victim in our own lives, so staying somewhere or with someone where suffering is your daily normal is not aiding your soul's growth in the least.

There's another old saying about god opening a window when he closes a door. It's actually your spirit guides who can perform that function for you, but you have to stop wallowing in anger and self-pity long enough to pause and listen to what they are trying to tell you.

Speaking of wallowing, I think we've spent enough time on dealing with negativity and how to identify it and eliminate or minimize it in our lives. Let's move on to talking about bringing in more positive energy.

If we're coming from a place of fairly pervasive negativity, and most of us are, the other side suggests starting to work in more positivity by adding it initially in a general sort of way. If you're starting a new job or entering a new relationship of any kind, start by expecting the best.

According to the universal law of attraction, you have to know what you don't want before you can know what you do want.

If you're coming out of a bad situation, you have certainly identified what you don't want in your life. Also, according to the same universal law, you get back whatever vibration you put out. If you always think, *I don't have a person in my life to love,* the universe will interpret that just as it's stated and will make sure you don't have a person in your life to love.

Our goal is to abandon negativity and move in a more positive direction. Even our thoughts have to be more positive. Say to the universe, "I know the person who will love me is out there—I just haven't met them yet." And don't try to put any time constraints on your new way of thinking. It happens when it happens—and often when you least expect it.

When I was impatiently waiting for something important to happen, Jasper popped in to say, "You want a time table? I'll give you a time table."

He showed me dozens of wristwatches attached to a long table and proceeded to smash them all to pieces with a large wooden mallet. He then said I should smash my own watch because things happen in their own time—and watching a clock and worrying doesn't make things happen any faster.

I didn't smash my watch, by the way, because I like it. I just stopped looking at it as often.

His point was that things we want to happen in our lives do so when they are supposed to, not on our time, no matter how hard we push.

In fact, good things most often happen when we stop trying to force them and let the universe take care of things.

Jasper suggests thinking of your life as going to a nice restaurant. You go in, sit down, place your order, and wait for your meal to be served. You don't place your order and then run back into the kitchen and start telling the chef how to cook it, or, even worse, start cooking it yourself.

You let the people who are trained to make your meal do their jobs, and the same is true of your soul guides. They are there to help you every step of the way if you will allow them to.

Now, where were we? We're turning our lives in a more positive direction by eliminating specific and then more general negative themes.

In turn, we are adding more general and then specific positivity, in that order, always bearing in mind through the entire process that we are the ones in total and absolute control of our emotions.

We have added general positivity by changing the background of our lives however we need to, be it involving a change in relationships or jobs, and we're ready to add daily specific positive things that keep us where we want to be spiritually.

The important thing about getting and keeping a positive attitude on a daily basis is building it out of a lot of little things so that if a few of them fade out over the course of the day, you still have enough other ones left to sustain your positivity. Don't let your positive attitude be dependent on just one thing being present or going the way you think it should.

I am admittedly not a morning person. It takes me a while to get into a positive mode, but sometimes, a song I like will pop into my head while I'm brushing my teeth, and I'll adopt that as the theme of the day.

A couple of days ago, Jasper showed up dressed in a tux like Frank Sinatra and started singing "The Best Is Yet to Come." I thought that was a great way to start the day. Even if you aren't currently in direct contact with the Jasper in your life, pick one of your own favorite songs and picture the artist singing it to you.

If you can get a good start on the day, the rest will flow more easily.

You can appreciate a good cup of coffee, a yummy doughnut, how beautiful the sky looks, or even give yourself a little pat on the back for being so good at what you do that you have a steady job to go to. The possibilities are endless.

You have the control, and you make the choice of how your day is going to go. When someone says, "Have a nice day," you can say, "Thanks. I've already decided I'm going to."

2

I'd Like to Buy a Vowel

I have been on an absolutely amazing spiritual journey for the past few years, and one of the things I learned that surprised me the most is the amount of aid and support available to us from the other side while we're incarnated here.

There is an unending supply of unconditional love from the creator, and we have our main soul guides, our emergency backup soul guides, our transitioned loved ones who may be waiting for us to get home so we can all start planning another life together, and seemingly any number of souls on the other side who may take a passing interest in giving us a little extra help when we need it.

During a recent session with Barb Ruhl, my mentor, we were sort of reviewing the events of the past three years and counting up the number of different energies from the other side that had shown us things along the way, and we found there have been dozens.

They may have been in the picture only briefly and perhaps had shown us something that was not entirely relevant to what we were learning at the time, but just the fact that I know they are there and taking an interest in what's happening in my earth life at the moment is very comforting.

Since every single one of us is on the same type of journey here, I know that all these energies are there for all of us. Barb and I are just two of the people who are fortunate enough to be able to see and hear them all clearly.

I'll get to how everyone who does not have as direct a connection can become more open to those communications a little later, but let's talk about the premise of this chapter first.

When I related the story of Lorna bringing the idea for a new initiative from the other side in the preface of this book, it was exciting and not at all surprising to me for the reasons I just discussed.

Ideas of all kinds to make life better or easier for us when we're incarnated are constantly being devised and developed on the other side and then sent to us through people who are tuned in to receive those particular vibrations, at a time when we are ready to hear them.

This particular new initiative, which Lorna said was to be called "Change a Letter, Change Your Life," is really a slightly different interpretation of the universal law of attraction, so before we can understand this variation of the law, we better discuss the law itself.

The idea of the law of attraction has been around since the late nineteenth century, but it has garnered a lot of attention in the past twenty-five years or so as one of the tenets of New Age thinking and philosophy.

It can be summarized by an old term we all learned in science class: like attracts like. If you prefer a more religious interpretation, it would be, you reap what you sow. In plain old everyday language, it is basically, you get back whatever you put out there.

As a better explanation, if you are constantly thinking negative thoughts about yourself and your life, then only negative things will be attracted to you. The same is true of positive thoughts.

For example, if you constantly think and say things like, "I never have enough money in the bank," the universe will hear that and make sure you get back exactly what it hears you saying, which is that you never want to have enough money in your bank account.

If you take a more positive attitude and say things like, "I may not have a lot of money in the bank, but I always have enough to pay my bills," then you will always have enough to pay the bills.

Many books have been written about the law of attraction.

Many authors have different perspectives on how to use the law to enhance your life, so I'm not going to go into it in any more depth here.

I want to focus on the new interpretation of the law Lorna has shared with us. If you want to learn more about the law from one viewpoint, a great teacher of the many facets of the law is Abraham Hicks, as interpreted by Esther Hicks. His lessons are available on line and are well worth your time.

Getting back to the piece of the law that Lorna wants us to focus on requires believing, and more importantly, believing without seeing.

It's about moving from a belief system that only accepts if-then as a basic truth to a system that acknowledges that when-then is the law.

One of our favorite catchphrases when we're incarnated here on earth is "I'll believe it when I see it." We all say it all the time, and we apply it to many of our life scenarios—everything from money, especially debts being repaid, to politics and politicians' promises, to our work lives, and everything in between.

It's only human to feel that way. We've all endured so many broken promises, both large and small, over the course of our lifetimes that it becomes natural to be cynical about everything and everybody.

The problem that arises is that by basing your belief system and living your life not believing in anything unless you can see, hear, touch, or smell it, you limit yourself to experiencing only those things that physically exist on this very small planet in this very small corner of the universe.

As I stated at the beginning of this chapter, the number of souls trying to help us through our earth lives from the other side is staggering, if we trust and believe they are there and allow them to help us.

The problem is, because you can't see or hear them in the usual human fashion, a lot of people find it hard to grasp even the concept that they all exist. If you can't believe, trust, and allow that they are there, it makes it very difficult for them to even try to offer you any assistance.

Enter Lorna. What she is telling us is to take that old saying "I believe when I see," and change the *w* in *when* to a *t,* which makes the phrase become, "I believe *then* I see." By doing that one simple thing, you activate the law of attraction in a more positive way rather than having it function in a mostly negative way.

You move from feeling like you're a victim in your own life to knowing that all your helpers on the other side are working in your best interest even if it isn't apparent to you at the time it is happening, and even if you are unaware of what your best interests may be.

Let's delve into my life story once again. Because I so enjoy dredging up my past—not. I only do it because I think using my fairly ordinary—up until a few years ago, anyway—life helps you, gentle reader, relate these ideas and concepts to your own life.

In my younger days, I changed jobs probably more frequently than most people my age because I hadn't learned to control my anger issues. About two years was all I could stand working in one place before I was fed up with everything connected with it.

At the end of the last century, after taking a job in another state and putting in my customary two years, I was looking to relocate back to my home state, preferably near where I had lived before. I knew I didn't want to go back to the employer I had left two years previously, but I wasn't sure what other jobs might be available in the area.

Out of the blue, an agency I had worked for occasionally called and asked if I might be interested in a permanent position that had just become available in a town very near to where I used to live. My answer was an immediate yes, the deal was sealed, and a few short weeks later, I was back where I wanted to be. Only for about two years, of course, but still where I thought I wanted to be.

The point of the story is this: all of this happened a long time before I regained my psychic abilities or had even heard of the law of attraction. I just knew I wanted to move back to where I had come from, and I believed there would be a job for me. Lo and behold, it happened.

If I had gone with my anger and fear-based negative thinking at the time, I would have been saying, "I'll never be able to find a job back there" or "I'll be stuck here forever," causing the law of attraction to be activated in a negative direction. I might still be where I didn't want to be.

Instead, Jasper takes retroactive credit for pushing me in the right direction. I believed I would find a way out of the situation, and I did. The universe responded to my belief with an unexpected phone call and a solution to the problem.

This might be a good place to change our focus a little and talk about some extremely important words that relate to activating the positive side of the law of attraction. They are simple words we all know and use frequently, but we need to understand them in slightly different ways than we are accustomed to in order to get the most benefit from our friends on the other side.

The first word is *believing*. "Believing without seeing," as Lorna told us. Even if you never see or hear directly from any of your spirit guides, or anybody else on the other side for that matter, you have to believe that they are there. You have to believe in the existence of something so much bigger than the brief life you are currently living on this small planet.

Try a simple thing like going outside at night and looking up at the star-filled sky. Even hard-core skeptics have to admit that the size of the universe is simply beyond human comprehension.

Even if every star you can see with the naked eye has only one planet orbiting that could sustain some kind of life form, the number of potentially inhabited planets is staggering.

Add to that the number of stars and galaxies than can only be seen with sophisticated telescopes, and once again, the number of potential life-bearing planets is beyond anything our puny human minds can comprehend.

These are tangible things you can observe for yourself, so in this case, you can see it, so there's no reason not to believe it.

The second word we have to bend the meaning of a little, which is closely related to believing, is *allowing*.

As I wrote in the last paragraph, everyone can see the stars at night and get some idea of the vastness of the universe, but you have to allow yourself to believe that in all that limitless space, there have to be other planets with other civilizations living out their lives just as we are here on earth.

Why do you have to allow yourself to believe it? Because we are all taught from the time we are children, especially those of us brought up in organized religion, that the god that controls the entire universe has only put people on this one little planet and is only concerned with making those people suffer during our one brief life here, and then taking joy in judging those same people after they die so he can consign them to heaven or hell.

How completely depressing that would be if it were in any way true. I like to call that kind of thinking "making god small."

It only serves the purpose of people trying to exert control over other people to not recognize that the universal source of unconditional love is big enough to be both the lubricant that keeps all the different parts of the universe working smoothly and the glue that binds it all together.

At the same time, that source is intimate enough with each of us to provide us with unconditional love and the strength to live out our many earthly incarnations and accomplish our learning goals.

Organized religion makes god small by teaching that he cares about what foods we eat on certain days, who we choose to love, or even what women are wearing to church.

By extricating yourself from these tired and erroneous beliefs, you can begin to allow a better understanding of the universe in a much broader scope.

As Shakespeare wrote more than five hundred years ago, "There are more things in heaven and earth, Horatio, than your philosophy allows." It's still valid, but a lot of people have yet to figure out how true it is.

It's obvious that even the thought of how organized religion continues to stifle spiritual growth when it should be encouraging it can get me up on my soapbox, so let me climb down and get back to the topic at hand, which is words we can use to activate the positive side of the law of attraction.

We've covered believing and allowing, which are sort of intertwined and accomplish the same goal of opening your mind enough to accept the existence of the other side and all the souls that are there to help us along in our spiritual journeys.

Trust is the next word that relates to the understanding we're trying to develop. Once you can allow yourself to believe that our friends on the other side are there to help us in any way they can, you have to trust that they will do just that.

This is one of the hardest things that all of us have to learn, especially if you're a recovering control freak like I am.

When you get yourself firmly into the believing/allowing mode, then you have to do what Jasper has referred to as "dropping the oars." At that point, your control issues can start to cause you all kinds of problems because you have to trust in your spirit guides to know better than you if you are heading in the right direction.

To give a more complete explanation of what "dropping the oars" really means, envision the earth life that you planned for yourself as a beautiful river.

Everything you wanted to come here to learn is providing the current that is carrying you along in your little life canoe, moving in the direction it should, which is always forward whether it seems that way or not.

There are occasional rapids and rough spots, but you planned for those too. There might even be times that you wrote into your life plan that the flow would stop or the river would be so shallow that you had to get out and carry your canoe over land until you got to a place where the water was deep enough and flowing again to get back in the canoe.

Regardless of the circumstances, your life is always flowing in the direction you planned for it to flow.

Here is where our human OCD control freak personalities step in to really screw things up.

When things are going too smoothly, we start questioning everything: Why does this seem so easy? Why are things going so well? Maybe I should try doing something different so things happen more quickly. That is when we can't help ourselves, and we stick our oars in the water, start paddling, and hope to change the way things are happening.

Good times or bad times, we have to start messing around with the flow of the grand plan to make something different start happening.

We either try to paddle downstream to make the good things come faster or paddle upstream to avoid facing the bad things that we planned to help us further our learning goals.

Learning to keep your oars out of the water and go with the flow is one of the hardest lessons we have to learn while we're incarnated.

Sometimes I think we placed the oars in our canoes to test ourselves. I know it was very hard for me to learn this lesson because I have a need to control everything. I still sometimes reach for the oars, but luckily, I have Jasper to smack my hands away before I can grab them.

The essence of the lesson is this: Our lives are already planned out by us before we incarnate. They have a flow that is not always smooth like we want it to be, but they flow in the direction we want to go. Putting the oars in the water and trying to paddle against or with the current only wastes your time and energy.

Your life, and indeed the universe at large, will unfold as it should, and paddling one way or the other from an issue doesn't mean you won't have to deal with it eventually.

It will go on your karma list for the next time around, so you might as well develop the coping skills for it now.

Perhaps more importantly, whenever you put those oars in the water and start paddling, you can activate the negative side of the law of attraction because any time your thoughts become overwhelmingly about what you don't want or don't have, the universe is only going to give you more of the same.

By not trying to move against the current, your canoe will naturally follow the path of least resistance and move in a positive downstream direction.

There couldn't be a better way to display your trust in the other side and in yourself than to be like the song from *Frozen* and "let it go."

You spent a great deal of time planning how you wanted this life to play out, and you put guides in place at home to help you accomplish your learning goals. Now, you should be able to just relax and let everyone do their jobs.

Trust me when I tell you that I don't think there was anyone else on the planet who believed more strongly in the old adage "If you want something done right, you have to do it yourself" than I used to.

I think it was an extension of my underlying OCD, and until I learned to trust in the universe and let my backstage crew do what they are there for, I didn't know how to let things flow. It's a difficult leap to make, but you must make it if you want to reach our final word, which is *freedom*.

Janis Joplin sang, "Freedom's just another word for nothing left to lose," and in a way, she was right. The lyric has a sort of negative connotation, but when used in a spiritual sense instead of a materialistic one, you can attain freedom by losing all the control issues you have about your life scenarios.

That spiritual type of freedom is what we are striving for, and once it is achieved, you've conquered your anger, fear, guilt, and doubts. There is nothing negative left to lose.

Spiritual freedom, real spiritual freedom, is less about having financial or worldly freedom and more about the feeling or emotion of freedom that you can experience anytime or place, regardless of your economic or social status.

Rather than conquering your fears, spiritual freedom might better be described as releasing your fears.

When you say you conquered your fear, that may be a tremendous achievement, but it may also mean that your fear is still lurking around in the background, waiting for an opportunity to rear its ugly head.

An even bigger achievement, and one that will lead to absolute spiritual freedom, is releasing your fears to the universe.

Allow the belief that fear isn't real—it's only a creation of your subconscious mind, and as such, it can be released to the universe, much like letting a helium-filled balloon go and watching it drift up and away in the breeze until it's out of sight.

Up until this point in human history, strong advocates for the existence and functioning of the law of attraction have tended to emphasize the piece of the law that focuses on bringing financial gain.

To be fair, it gets the attention of a lot of people if you tell them they have untold riches available to them if they will only believe it's there and ask the universe in the right way to release it to them.

Teaching the law of attraction in that way fails to emphasize that the whole thing is not about the money, though it's great when it does come through. It's about the emotion attached to having "enough" money, whatever that may mean to many different people.

That emotion is a feeling of freedom from worrying about never having enough money.

There are two reasons I focus on the financial freedom aspect of the law: first, because it is the most taught and talked about part of it, and second, I, like millions of others, always felt that if I only had a big pile of money, I would be free of worrying about paying the bills, free of having to go to work every day, and be free to live exactly as I wanted to.

After everything I've learned, though I can't deny that it seems like it would be great to have that big pile of money, I know that I am free in so many more ways that financial freedom becomes a smaller part of the picture.

Let's count up some of the ways we are free. First, and maybe foremost, we are free to stop worrying about our present incarnation here on earth. Everything in our lives has been planned out in advance, and if we can only allow that simple idea to enter our consciousness, we can stop struggling and go with the flow. Everything will unfold as it should.

Second, we are free to stop worrying what happens to us when we "die." As I wrote in my last book, we simply leave these bodies, and the essence of who we are goes home. Easy-peasy, mac and cheesy.

Third, we are free to decide how we're going to feel about and react to everything that is happening in our life scenarios. Once we learn to get rid of and/or control all the anger, fear, and guilt in our lives, everything seems to flow much more easily.

Up until the past few years, I was one of those people who used to constantly think things like, *I hate getting up and going to work in the morning, I hate my job, I can't stand doing this much longer,* and *Why can't I hit the lottery to end this misery?*

It would start every Sunday afternoon when I entered what I called my "prework depression." As the day wore on, I would get crankier and crankier, just thinking about how much I would hate getting up on Monday morning to go to a place I didn't want to go and doing something I didn't want to do.

I was wasting half the weekend worrying about the next week.

What I failed to realize was, if I decided I was going to be miserable before I even got to work, of course I would be miserable the whole day after I got there. I was telling the universe I wanted to be unhappy, so using the negative side of the law of attraction, I was being given exactly what I was asking for. Duh.

I'm not going to sugarcoat it and tell you that making any of these changes in thinking is easy, especially when you've been running that same old program in your head for a lot of years. I will tell you that I managed to do it, and if I can, anyone can.

I moved away from the dark side of the force and replaced my negative thinking with positive thoughts.

I'm not saying I turned into Rebecca of Sunnybrook Farm or that I always feel like everything is sunshine, lollipops, and rainbows, but instead of deciding I'm going to have a terrible day before I even get to work, I take baby steps in a positive direction.

I think about having a good day and enjoying the people I will be working with. If it's really busy, I'll think, *Wow, the day is really going fast. It's already lunchtime,* or *One more hour, and I get to go home.*

Change your thoughts to anything that will help turn off all that negativity and turn in even a little bit more positive direction. Shoot for something neutral if you can't get all the way to positive at first. Always remember to start with baby steps.

Once you have conquered the day-to-day negativity, and maybe even banished the prework depression without resorting to drugs and alcohol, you can focus on the bigger picture.

Start imagining what it would feel like not to have to work at that particular place at all. Begin saying things to yourself like, "It will feel great when I don't have to work here anymore" or "It will feel great when I don't have to do this work ever again." Allow yourself to experiment with those good feelings.

Thinking those types of things will activate the positive side of the law of attraction, and the universe may bring you a promotion, a new job, or even a new career that you hadn't seen on your radar before.

How can any of this be as easy as it seems? Can I really change my whole life by changing the way I think about simple everyday things?

It is as easy as believing, allowing, and trusting, but it is also as difficult as believing, allowing, and trusting.

We have to let go of all the old programming that has been instilled in us since we were children and ignore a great deal of our life experience to be able to change the *w* in *when* I see to the *t* in *then* I see.

Jasper says that when people are incarnated, for some reason, we become obsessed with lists and having everything laid out in order to show us which way to go. He gave me a five-step program for working toward our goal of changing our thinking:

1. Understand that looking only at your current reality calls attention to the fact that whatever you want is not there.

2. Use your current reality to provide a desire for change by thinking more and more about what you do want to be included in it.

3. After you decide what exactly it is you do want, put in a work order for it with your guides.

4. Trust the universe to take care of the situation—and don't ask for what you want repeatedly. Asking for the same thing over and over shows a lack of trust.

5. After you have put in your request, stop staring at and obsessing over your current reality. Go back to step one and read it again.

Jasper just showed up dressed in a beautiful long evening gown like the ones worn by Ms. Vanna White on *Wheel of Fortune*. Believe me, Vanna, you don't have to be afraid of the competition. He's trying to turn the letter on the puzzle board to make the *w* in when to a *t*, but it's stuck and won't turn. Now he has his high heel braced against it and is trying to pry it loose. It's quite a scene.

Anyway, his point is, I think, that it's not easy to change something that is a core belief for many people. It will take work and some struggle. But just as on *WOF*, if you can manage to get the letters turned in the right way, you can win some great prizes—one of which is a whole new outlook on life.

A Star Is Born

A Star is Born is one of those great old movies, like so many others, originally made in the 1940s. It starred Bette Davis as an established but fading movie star who takes a young actress under her wing and ends up having most of her life stolen from her by said starlet in the process.

It's worth watching just to hear Ms. Davis deliver one of the most famous lines of dialogue in movie history: "Fasten your seat belts—it's going to be a bumpy ride."

The main theme of the movie is that trusting seemingly innocent people who want to be close to you may not always be such a good idea.

The premise may not be exactly relevant to anything we're discussing in this book, but that famous line about being prepared for a bumpy ride certainly is. It is especially apropos to my relationship with Jasper, my main soul guide.

On December 18, 2013, he made his presence known to me for the first time—and I've needed my seat belt fastened ever since. That date, by the way, has been designated (by himself, of course) as Intergalactic Jasper Day. International Jasper Day would be too small an event for the celebration of someone of his stature.

By giving the world access to his immense store of knowledge and his considerable charm, I have allowed a new star to be born. Have I mentioned that Jasper has custody of nearly all the self-esteem we're supposed to be sharing during this incarnation?

The reason I relate all my Jasper experiences to you, gentle reader, other than that he loves being the center of attention, is to let you know that just because he enjoys being the man of a thousand faces with accompanying costume changes doesn't mean any other guide in the universe will be like him.

He uses his over-the-top behavior as an avenue to show and teach me things in the way I need to be shown and taught. His methods were worked out by both of us before I incarnated for this life, and with good reason.

In December 2013, I was sixty years old, not very happy, and had essentially decided that my life was just about over. All I wanted to do was figure out a way to retire and then sit around and wait to die. My spiritual growth and learning had pretty much stopped, and I felt like there wasn't much left to look forward to.

Then on the thirteenth day of that fateful month came the boom. There was Jasper, looking for all the world like Al from Al's Diner on *Happy Days* and projecting such energy that it was impossible not to see, hear, and feel him. In the years since, he has used his wit and imagination to teach me many things about life and living, and I'm using books like this one to pass that knowledge on to you.

Yes, folks, to increase both my knowledge and understanding as well as yours, I have endured all of his name-calling and abuse as he tries time and again to pour his wisdom into my puny human mind.

Actually, that's not entirely true. I would do it all again even if it was for me and me alone.

My life has done a 180 from what it was before I knew he was there all the time, and instead of waiting to die, I can't wait to find out what else I have to learn before I finally go home. I've replaced my fear and dread of growing old with excitement about learning and growing spiritually until my last day on earth.

Do I credit meeting Jasper with turning my life around? Not completely, much to his dismay. I always bear in mind that I am the one who planned my life the way it is and was.

I put in the sixty years of some not-very-happy scenarios in order to learn various lessons and coping skills. I do give him a lot of credit for hanging in there through the times I didn't even know he existed.

Looking back and thinking it over, I can see more than a few occasions when he helped point me in the right direction, and he even saved me from death or injury in a few car accidents.

This is the truth that everyone needs to work on allowing. Even when you don't know that your spirit guides are there, or if you acknowledge their existence but have never seen or heard them, or know their names, they are there.

We all have binding agreements with them made before we incarnate stating that they will be with us from cradle to grave and do their absolute damndest to keep us on the life plan we've written for ourselves.

You may live your entire life without having direct contact with any of your guides, but there should be no doubt that they are there and helping you as much as they can from behind the scenes.

At this point, you may be wishing I would just shut up about Jasper, but I can't.

First and foremost, he wouldn't allow it, and secondly and more importantly, he is the teacher this time around and I am the student, which makes all of you reading this book his students by default, so you have to go along for the ride.

The thing you really have to know about Jasper is that, for better or worse, he is mine and mine alone. He and I are both happy to share his antics when they are useful as teaching tools, but his primary residence is in my head, even though my colleague Barb can see and hear him most of the time.

I'm not telling you this to make you jealous, though I'm not sure many of you would be anyway. I'm trying to make the point that all of us have our own soul guides, and just as we are all unique and individual, so are they.

Before we incarnate, we enter into an agreement with our individual guide that they will be with us our entire lives and will assume the personality that will be most helpful to us while we live out our incarnations.

For Jasper and me, that meant he would be loud and animated to get and keep my attention. Barb's guide, Ella, on the other hand, is very calm and low-key, which counteracts some of Barb's high energy. Most of the guides I have been able to have contact with have personalities that fit nicely with the personalities of the incarnated person they are working with. Sort of a yin-yang kind of dovetailing.

To get back to the lesson that Jasper is trying to teach us, we have to go to the theater. He has told us before that we are the stars of our own little life dramas, and everyone we interact with during our earth lives are our costars and the bit players in the piece.

He also explained how our guides and friends at home could be considered backstage workers, creating all the scenery and props, and making sure the lighting is correct so that everything works together to produce the play composed of all our life scenarios.

When we have finished our current life play, the curtain simply comes down, and there is an intermission while everything backstage is changed and rearranged. All the actors regroup and rehearse a new play, the curtain goes up, and the whole thing starts again.

I wrote at length about how our lives are very similar to stage plays in one of my previous books, and I thought I had a pretty good understanding of the lesson Jasper was trying to teach me with that analogy, but with my puny human mind and all, I missed a very important point. Let me explain it now and get us all up to speed.

While everything I wrote about us being the stars of our own life plays, and our guides being the backstage crew is true and correct, because we are human and live here in the mess that is planet earth, we can royally screw up our own performances.

We all have control issues to a greater or lesser degree, and it can take a long time for us to learn the whole believe/trust/allow thing I wrote about in the last chapter. For those very human reasons, it's tough to concentrate on our primary jobs of being the star.

Not to mention that those of us with self-esteem issues feel we have no business being the star. We can't believe that when the curtain goes up, the backstage crew will have everything in place and ready: the scenery will be painted, the props will be in place, and the lighting will be correct.

The problem that arises from not trusting that the crew has done and will be doing their jobs correctly is that we're not out front and on center stage where we should be and need to be when the curtain goes up.

We have to be there to make the production flow smoothly; otherwise, we're basically absent from pieces of our own lives. It would be like watching one of those old movies where they keep playing the same music over and over, waiting for the star of the show to make an entrance.

As Jasper is so fond of telling me: You have one job, now don't screw it up. Your one and only job is to be the star of your own life.

No actor on Broadway gives a second thought to what the backstage people are doing. They know they are professionals and that everything they need to perform the scene perfectly will be where it needs to be when the curtain goes up.

The star only has to worry about hitting their marks and speaking the right dialogue. The backstage crew takes care of everything else.

It's not like one of those old Judy Garland/Mickey Rooney "let's put on a show in the barn" movies where Judy and Mickey clean out the barn, build the stage, paint the scenery, and still have enough energy left to be adorable and star in the show. Our guides give us one job—be the star—so we have to try our best to fill that role.

Since this chapter deals with my relationship with Jasper (and he's loving it) and how we communicate, for those of you who are unaware, one of his favorite teaching tools is using old movies and TV shows to get his point across. To give a little deeper explanation of the way our guides help us move forward spiritually, he wants us to think of that great old movie, *The African Queen*, starring Katherine Hepburn and Humphrey Bogart.

For those of you who haven't seen the movie, first of all, your cultural education is severely lacking, and secondly, it's about the captain of an African riverboat, played by Humphrey Bogart. He agrees to take a missionary, played by Katherine Hepburn, on a dangerous trip to escape from the Germans during World War I. Along the way, they face many dangers and end up falling in love.

After a brief discussion with Jasper about which of us would be assuming which role, it was decided that, for this lesson, I could be Bogie, and he would be Katherine, which I have a strong suspicion he wanted to be all along. But back to the plot, which we have to twist a little to make it fit what we're learning.

In the movie, Bogie controls the direction of the ship, and Katherine provides encouragement and as much help as she can.

In our spiritual lives, our guides are controlling the engine and rudders, and we, as the captains of our little ship, are standing at the prow and directing the guides on which way to point the ship and at what speed.

We can ask their advice about which fork in the river to take, but we are always in control of the direction our life is taking and where we're headed. Even though our guides have access to our entire life plans and know we should be going one way instead of the other, they will turn the rudder to point the ship in whatever direction we decide, a decision that is often influenced by whatever we happen to be focusing on at the moment.

If we are looking at what we don't want or don't have, even if it's on the riverbank, they will run us aground if we tell them to go that way. On the other hand, if we are focused on what we do want, which is forward progress in our spiritual journey, they will happily steer us to open water.

This is a really good explanation of how everything in the universe, our soul guides included, must obey the law of attraction. If we choose to see only negatives, they will steer us toward them, but if we focus on positivity and moving forward, they will have to take us there. Even though they are steering the ship, they only respond to whatever commands we are giving.

We are always in complete control of our lives, whether we choose to believe it or not. We are the ones to decide if we are going to hit the iceberg or steer clear. Wait, that's from *Titanic*. Jasper needs to learn to keep his movie metaphors straight. And, no, I will not be Rose so he can be Jack.

The point is, I think, that we can look at the relationship we have with our guides in a lot of different ways, but what we need to know and remember is that they are there twenty-four seven, and they love us unconditionally.

They will never do anything to push us into doing something stupid. We can manage to do that very well on our own. They are what many consider to be angels, providing us with guidance and support even when we're not aware they are doing it.

For all they do for us, we are still controlling the direction our lives will take, and in spite of our sometimes feeling we have been abandoned during a rough patch, we are never alone.

4

Auntie Em, It's a Twister

The purpose of this entire book, I've come to realize, is to provide you, the reader, with multiple options for changing the way you think about life.

By doing that, our friends on the other side say that at least one of the explanations will resonate with someone and you will actually be able to change your life for the better by using the information they are giving.

They recently shared are very interesting analogy with Barb and me, which I will relate here.

When we plan our lives before we incarnate, we have a tendency to stick a lot of negativity in there, usually against the advice of everyone on the other side who is helping us in the actual planning.

When we're incarnated, we have that amnesia about how wonderful things are at home, and when at home, we have a measure of amnesia about how bad things can get while we're living out our earth lives.

Our goal is ever and always to learn as much as we possibly can during these lives to aid in our spiritual growth, so it's only natural to want to experience as many negative scenarios as we can possibly pack into our short earth lives.

For that reason, we often bite off more than we can chew during the planning stage, and by the time we get to adulthood on this side, a lot of us are not coping well.

In fact, some of us are so far from coping that we are approaching a state of near hysteria, basically running through our lives with our hands in the air and screaming like Macaulay Culkin in *Home Alone.*

If we allow ourselves to get to that extreme place where we are feeling a loss of control over everything, it feels like we are living in the middle of that proverbial shit storm.

No matter what we try to do, or which way we turn, bad and smelly things just keep hitting us in the face and prevent us from seeing any way out. To keep from offending the more sensitive among us, going forward, I will refer to this uniquely human predicament as a fecal tornado.

Actually, our lives are designed by us to include all types of weather: sunshine and storms, and even the occasional tornado, but manageable ones.

If we didn't want to experience all the different types of negativity that are always present on the earth plane, and learn from them by living through them, we could stay at home.

It is always an option to watch all the brave souls—I almost wrote *masochists*—who choose to come here from the comfort and safety of the other side while they struggle, suffer, and learn from firsthand experience.

I'm sure we all know people who are living one of those charmed lives where nothing bad ever seems to happen to them, and nothing ever seems to go wrong, but is that actually what is going on? Is the reality that they are like ducks, calm and serene above the surface, but paddling like hell under the water?

No one can ever really know what anybody else is living through, though a lot of people spend an inordinate amount of time trying to second-guess and criticize other people's lives when they should be spending time coping with their own issues.

Worrying about the piece of sawdust in someone else's eye while ignoring the plank in your own is a classic bait and switch that allows you to delay and avoid dealing with your own problems. By doing that, however, you stop all your own personal spiritual growth.

One of the things we're going to be learning about in a later chapter is redefining the word *selfish* to remove the negative connotation. All growth and learning have to start with a self-examination and the realization that you can't live anybody's life but your own.

Being jealous of someone who seems to have the perfect life isn't going to make your life any better. Maybe they planned to have a calm and peaceful life this time just to see what that would be like. Or perhaps they are like our web-footed friends and are struggling in private but refusing to show it in public.

Whatever the case, the important point is to keep your eyes on your own paper because you can't pass the exam by cheating from someone else's answers. Everyone writes their own test, so you have to answer your own questions.

But to get back to our weather-related analogy, the bottom line is this: if your life doesn't make you feel like you're spinning in a tornado from time to time, you probably aren't learning very much in the way of coping skills. It's only by developing those skills that you learn how to step out of the swirling winds and into the calm eye at the center of the storm.

I'm getting a little ahead of myself, so let me back up and present the imagery exactly the way it was presented to Barb and me.

You are living your current earth life, not coping very well with all the negativity you planned for yourself when it comes along, and you've reached the point where you are indeed feeling like Kevin in *Home Alone*, in your mind, if not actually physically.

The way you are dealing with your problems is by running around, waving your hands in the air, and screaming hysterically.

Other than a spot-on Macaulay Culkin as an eight-year-old impersonation, what exactly are you accomplishing there? I'd have to say nothing of any educational value because even if you do a great job, I seriously doubt it's going to get you to the final round on *America's Got Talent*.

At this point, you are inhabiting only the very top of the fecal tornado and are just going around and around in circles with no control over the direction of your life. If you can stop the screaming for a few minutes, what can you do to get out of this mess?

That is a very good question because acknowledging that things have gotten out of control is the important first realization you must come to before you can start to change. You know things don't feel right, and negative scenarios seem to keep repeating in your life.

You wonder why bad things keep happening to you. The reason that the same "bad" things keep reappearing is that you are stuck in the top of that tornado, going around in circles. By not learning to cope with them, you are allowing them to keep coming back into your life.

Let's use something simple that a lot of us can relate to: hating your job. You feel trapped, but not in a bad job like you think you are, but in the emotion of hate that you are allowing yourself to feel about the job.

You're stuck in the top of the tornado, which is the hatred of your job, and like Helen Hunt in *Twister*, every Monday morning brings a big old cow with "job" painted on its side swirling toward you. Of course, you can't avoid the cow, even though you see it coming, because your hatred of the cow keeps you fixated on the pain it's going to cause.

But who is really to blame for the pain? Is it poor old Bossy that got sucked up into your tornado—or is it you because you haven't learned to cope with all your negative feelings about her? I think you know the answer.

By facing the situation, which is that Bossy is going to be in your tornado no matter what, because you have to have a job to pay the bills, the only things you can control and change are your feelings about the old girl.

It may seem that controlling and changing—maybe a better word would be *managing*—your emotional responses toward something or someone would be very difficult. In reality, all it takes is some insight into yourself and how you act and react in certain situations to get you started.

Let's think about that job. Why do you hate it so much? Is it what you do, the people you work with, or the way you are treated by your boss? Could it even be something like the location of your job or even the building your job is in?

There has to be a central and primary reason why you hate going there every day. You have to take the time to think about it and figure out the reason behind your hatred.

For the sake of argument, let's say you ponder the matter and decide that you really like what you do, you like most of the people you work with, even your boss, but the company you work for has so many policies and procedures you can't agree with that the negative feelings about that part of your job are canceling out the positive feelings you have about the other parts of your job.

This is great news! Now that you know you're allowing what you feel about maybe 25 percent of your job to color the way you feel about the other 75 percent, you can start to minimize the negative part and maximize the positive part.

As Bing Crosby and the Andrews sisters sang during World War II (fire up the Google, children), you've got to "ac-cen-tu-ate the positive and e-lim-in-ate the negative." I knew I had that song in my head lately for a reason! It can be a simple as that, if you let it.

Focus on how much you enjoy what you do and the people you do it with rather than the conditions you have to do it under.

Is there any way to work on changing the policies you don't like? If there is, then get yourself on the committee that makes policy decisions and work for change. If the policies are carved in stone and can't or won't be changed, then why do you let yourself get angry and crazy about them? All that does is make you angry and crazy.

You can never change something you don't have the power to change. The only things you have the power to change in this world are yourself, your emotions, and the way you react to the scenarios you encounter. That's the key.

Since all spiritual growth and learning depends on each of us having a complete understanding and acceptance of the concept, the only things you have the complete power to control are the way you view the scenarios you're living through and your emotional reactions to those situations.

Only you can decide if it's worth your time and energy to hate somebody or something you know you can never change. Most of the people we don't like could care less how we feel about them anyway, much less changing how they act just to make us happy.

We have to make our own happiness, and if that means having no further contact with some people or places in our lives, then so be it.

Everything the guides are trying to teach us in this book is about moving away from our self-imposed feelings if victimhood and into feeling empowered and free because we deserve to feel that way. A lot more of that will come in future chapters, so let's get back to the current lesson, which is managing the fecal tornado that our lives can become if we allow it.

Returning to our job-hating premise, once you've figured out exactly what it is about your job you don't like and have adjusted your emotional response as much as you feel you possibly can, you may decide that you can't deal with being there long term.

At that point, it's probably time to look for another job.

Since you're in a more positive frame of mind, you can actually practice feeling the positive emotions that would come from getting that new and better job. Instead of the constant litany of, "I hate my job," try saying, "I really enjoy what I do, and I know it will feel great when I'm doing it somewhere that I feel accepted and valued."

This is part and parcel of the law of attraction that we're learning about. If your thoughts are only about how much you hate your job, then all the universe is going to give you is more hate for your job.

If you can flip that emotion and start getting excited about how great a new job is going to feel, then the universe will work to bring you that new job.

But let's get back to the analogy comparing our lives to that fecal tornado. We're going to say that we've worked through the hysteria over the negativity in our lives and have it under control enough that we can look down from the top of the funnel and see the center or eye of the storm and want to be in that calm.

We're in a place where we realize that the calm spot actually exists, we get glimpses of it from time to time, and we know instinctively that we want to be in it. We know we have to work our way down there, but how?

We've made huge progress by learning to identify the negative feelings in our lives because when we see that cow spinning toward us, and it's labeled job or money or relationships, we can get out of the way by moving ourselves downward in the tornado and closer to the eye of the storm. All we have to do is change our perception of the problem to a more positive one than we currently have.

Once we've learned exactly what it is that makes us afraid, angry, or guilty, we can deal with it directly. We're learning coping skills, and the added weight of that knowledge in our emotional toolboxes is helping us work our way to the bottom of the swirling winds and into the calm at the center.

When we get into the eye, it doesn't mean the tornado stops spinning. Life and all the craziness that goes with it aren't going to stop moving all around us. It just means we'll be able to stand still, catch our breath, and watch it go around us for a while.

At first, while we're still working on developing and mastering our coping skills, the eye of the storm will be small. There will really just be room enough for us to stand there. If we so much as stick out a pinkie, we can get sucked back into the whirlwind and be sent all the way back to the top, where the hysteria lives, to start over.

Since we've at least started to develop new coping skills, our descent into the eye of the storm takes less and less time with every trip. And every time we get to the eye, it gets wider and wider until the whole tornado changes from a funnel shape to a cylinder shape that gives us plenty of room to stand in the calm permanently if we choose to.

I don't know how I managed to get this far without referencing Jasper's favorite movie, *The Wizard of Oz*. I didn't mention seeing Elvira Gulch on her bicycle as we descended through the tornado or make any remarks about dropping a house on anyone's sister. Amazing. But don't worry, we have a whole chapter about that movie coming up.

There is one important comparison he would like to make, though, and that is this: during the course of our spiritual journeys here on earth, we often feel like the scarecrow after he was attacked by the flying monkeys. There's a piece of us over there, another piece of us over there, and our stuffing may be falling out. It seems, at times, that we will never be whole again.

But just like Ray Bolger, pieces of us may be scattered everywhere, but we have the knowledge that we are always in direct contact with the unconditional love of the creator, and that the lives we're living are ones we planned for the purpose of learning and aiding our soul's growth.

Even in the worst of times, when we feel like we're being torn apart by the flying monkeys, it's all going according to plan— and everything will turn out as it should.

Wow, Jasper! Thanks for that. It almost brought a tear to my eye. Perhaps he's going to start showing me a new, kinder gentler side of himself!

No, it must have been a momentary lapse because I'm back to getting the same old eye rolls. I think he's really a softie, but he doesn't want me to see that side of him. I guess we'll all find out as things continue to unfold for both of us!

5

I Reject Your Reality and Replace It with My Own

I was born and raised in a small town in the mountains of Western Pennsylvania. Some might have considered it to be northern West Virginia, but I like to think of it as Appalachia adjacent. Whatever you choose to call it, it was very rural and very isolated, and it was full of good, hardworking, regular people.

After I grew up and moved to a somewhat more urban area, I used to have a good time at work regaling my coworkers with stories about my assorted aunts, uncles, and cousins and their antics, which, seemed completely normal to me when I was growing up.

I didn't know anything different, and pretty much all families in my little town were like mine.

I can remember when reality shows like *I Didn't Know I Was Pregnant* first appeared on television. When the conversation about that show started, I would say, "Yeah, that happened to one of my cousins." And the shows kept appearing: *America's Most Wanted*? Yeah, I think I saw one of my cousins on there. *16 And Pregnant*? It goes without saying.

Finally, one day, my friend at work said, "Is there anything that hasn't happened to one of your relatives?" I had to stop and think for a minute, but I finally said, "I don't think any of them have ever admitted to being abducted by aliens, but some of them may actually be aliens."

That was a long time ago, and unfortunately, most of the family that led such interesting lives and provided the material for such great stories have died off from one thing or another. I'm left with only the memories of them—or at least as much as I can recall.

There is an old saying "up home," as we always called it once we moved away, that when someone takes as long to get to the point of a story as I am with this one, that they were "going around the barn to get to the house," so let me tie up these loose ends.

One of the stars in the cast of characters that made up my extended family was an aunt who could best be described as a free spirit.

She had many talents, but one of her most notable was yodeling, which she would be happy to do with only the slightest bit of encouragement, and sometimes with no prompting at all.

I remember my in-laws from the big city falling over laughing when she grabbed the microphone and cut loose during my mother's second wedding reception. Alcohol consumption may have been a factor, but it was entertaining nonetheless.

I'm bringing up yodeling because it provides a pretty vivid mental picture of someone on a Swiss mountaintop calling out, "Yo-de-lay-hee-hoo," and then hearing the same phrase echoed back from the valley below.

Got that image in your mind? Great.

Now place yourself on that mountain and imagine you are yodeling, "Yo-de-man I want isn't here." You can make up your own clever phrase about whatever you think is missing from your life and wait for the echo to come back to you. And what will that echo be? Exactly the same sentiment you just yodeled!

That's what an echo is—the noise you made coming back to you.

After all that, you can surely see through my clever little ruse to try to explain the law of attraction in a slightly different way.

Consider the universe to be one giant echo chamber that will send back to you whatever words you are putting out there, whether they are positive or negative. For that reason, the way you frame your thoughts is very important to activating the law to send you in the direction you want to go.

Your brain and your thoughts are the things that are most closely connected to the other side and the souls there that are trying to help and guide us.

If your thoughts are constantly negative or you dwell on whatever you think is lacking in your life most of the time, the law of attraction says that those types of thoughts will be received by the universe as being the things you desire most.

For that reason, the echo you receive back from the universe will be a reinforcement of your negativity. The same holds true for positive thoughts.

To provide a more specific example, let's talk about money, which, along with relationships, seems to be the biggest concern of most people on the planet today.

Many, many people are working as hard as they can and still can't seem to be able to get ahead financially. Sound familiar? If you feel that you are always in a similar situation, what are the thoughts you have about money? I never have enough money in the bank. I'll never be able to afford that new car or house. I can't afford a vacation, a new dress, or a Starbucks latte.

They are all negative. They all contain words like *can't* and *never*.

The universe hears your thoughts and says, "Okay, for whatever reason, this person never wants to have enough money in the bank or have a new car or house. Done."

You will never have what you consider to be enough money because you have told the universe repeatedly that is the way you want it.

You have to do a 180 with those thoughts and get rid of all the cant's and nevers. You have to alter your thinking to say, "I do have enough money in the bank to pay the bills," and before you know it, you will.

You may think, *I'd really like to be able to afford a Starbucks today*, and then put on a coat you haven't worn in a while and find a ten-dollar bill in the pocket.

Start changing your every thought about money from the negative, "I never have enough" to the positive, "I do have enough to pay the bills this month," and see what happens.

It won't cost anything to change the way you think, and it certainly doesn't require any physical exertion. You just have to be mindful of your thought processes.

When you hear yourself thinking about your needs and desires in a way that emphasizes the absence of those things, stop the thought and turn it in a more positive direction.

With all that being said, you have to be realistic about the positive thoughts you put out there. As Jasper so bluntly says,

"Don't be stupid. Just because you have positive thoughts about a Lamborghini being in your driveway when you get home from work doesn't mean it will happen."

You have to think in more general terms and remember that all change starts with baby steps in the right direction. Ask your friends on the other side to start showing you scenarios that will help you get to the place you want to be, which in this example is being able to afford to buy a Lamborghini.

They may start showing you ways to increase your income, perhaps a new job or new career path you hadn't considered before. Ask them to let you feel what it would be like to tool around town in a very expensive car and then practice having those emotions.

After having the feeling of owning that car, you may find that it isn't about the car at all. It's more about having the freedom to be able to buy something like that without sacrificing your financial independence.

It's very important to have goals and ask the guides to help you move toward them, but they say that often when you get to where you think you want to go, you find out you want to go somewhere else, so you never actually reach your goal because it is always changing.

That's what makes the whole incarnating-for-a-life-here thing fun and interesting. It's a giant game where the finish line keeps moving. All we have to do is learn the rules spelled out in the law of attraction, and we will never get bored by having to play the same old game over and over.

Of course, there is plenty of help from the other side.

In *Jerry Maguire,* Tom Cruise is talking to Cuba Gooding, Jr. on the phone and keeps saying, "Help me help you!" Your guides are playing that scene in a continuous loop. The only reason they are there is to help you help yourself get through this life you planned.

All it takes is for us watch and listen for the signs they give us all the time that most of us choose to ignore. Those signs can take many forms, and some are more obvious than others.

If you are looking for a way to make more money, you may overhear people talking at work or in a restaurant about a job opportunity that may be of interest to you. You may even get a phone call or email out of the blue like I did.

You may be walking down a street you don't usually travel, but you had a feeling you should go that way today, and you see a Help Wanted sign in a window. Maybe you decided to read the newspaper for some reason, even though you don't usually, and you read about an opportunity in there.

Try to listen and look for even the tiniest messages and signs that the universe may be sending. Go with the flow and accept any help you feel is coming from the other side.

People sometimes ask how they can tell if the message is from their guides. The answer is simple. If it's a positive and loving message, it's from them. They are incapable of being negative, so if it doesn't feel quite right, it's your subconscious trying to influence your decision.

Always remember that, first and foremost, you planned everything that is happening in your life before you came here. Stop looking for someone to blame for the parts of it you don't like. Remember that your guides and everyone else who is helping you on the other side are your friends—not your parents.

When we come into our earth lives, we need a parent or parents to shepherd us along while we grow up. Often, we will have worked with them on the other side during the planning stage and given them instruction to treat us in certain ways during childhood so we can learn whatever we want to learn this time around.

From my own experience, I planned to have my father basically ignore me and my mother treat me rather badly so I could work on learning patience, tolerance, forgiveness, and how to restore your self-esteem when it's sucked out of you on a pretty much daily basis.

Yeah, I know, I'm a glutton for punishment, but it worked—and it made me realize how much my mother had to love me to agree to live a life as a person who was the polar opposite of who she really is.

And that brings me to the moral of the story, which is that parents, and all the grief that they can cause, only exist in this dimension, and they only exist to help the souls that incarnate here learn the lessons they want to learn.

The one overarching thing that almost all parents teach is that love is conditional, unfortunately, or fortunately for the purposes of soul growth. It is a very rare parent who will say to a young child, "You have a choice: if you do this, then we're good, but if you do that, you will be punished." The vast majority will just react to whatever the child does with some form of punishment, reinforcing the idea that if everything is not done the parents' way, then love will be withheld and punishment given.

For just about everybody, receiving love from outside ourselves becomes contingent on whatever conditions the person you want to receive that love from establishes. If it's from your parents, the giving of love will be based on conditions like cleaning your room, finishing your homework, or doing any of the hundreds of other things that go into the raising of a functional human being.

As we get older, girlfriends and boyfriends—followed by wives and husbands—put all kinds of conditions on the giving of love. It's no wonder that we can lose sight of even the meaning of unconditional love as it exists on the other side.

Luckily, our friends at home are in a state of unconditional love with us and everything in the universe. When they are guiding and trying to advise us, they are unconditional in every imaginable way.

They are unconditional trust, support, and guidance. They are like the best of friends we have in this dimension if we are fortunate enough to have them. You know the ones I mean. The friends who when you say you are going to do something really stupid or dangerous will first say, "Are you sure?" When you say, "I'm sure," they say, "Then I'm in!"

As Jasper says, your guides are with you unconditionally—even if you choose to be unconditionally stupid.

That pretty much sums up my current thoughts on reality, and the thing I have come to learn is that there really is no such thing as reality.

Life as we know it here is an illusion. Our real lives are at home on the other side, and we pop in and out of these earthly incarnations like kids playing dress up. We take on different roles at different times for the enhancement of our learning of coping skills, which enhances our soul growth and aids in the expansion of the universe.

How's that for a New Agey paragraph? I know it will sound like gibberish to many people, and until a few years ago, it would have sounded that way to me also.

My point, and like Ellen says, I do have one, is that learning to change the way you have been thinking about how you approach life since you were a child takes time—often a lot of time.

Progress can seem to be made at a glacial pace, many times with the old three steps forward and two steps back thrown in to further complicate things. Jasper keeps emphasizing baby steps. You have to walk before you can run. Rome wasn't built in a day. Add any of your own platitudes about patience that you can think of.

You have to be committed and willing to change to have the patience to let the change happen. The other side has given us a short list of three things that we have to deal with as we try to change those old programs running through our heads.

First, we have to conquer the fear of change. It may sound easy, but it's a pretty big topic that can mean many different things to different people.

On examination, the fear has its roots in not knowing what changing your thought patterns will bring. What if you don't like your life after you make a change? What if you don't like yourself after you change? The obvious answer is you can always change back to the way you were or change into something completely different.

Unfortunately, just like Garth in *Wayne's World*, we fear change, and the thought of going through it is terrifying to some people.

The truth is, change is one of the few constants in our lives. Everything around us is changing all the time. It has to be—or we would still be living in caves, and it would be pointless to keep reincarnating into the same scenarios over and over.

Fear is also a key component in the second thing on our list that we need to do: stop caring about what other people and the world at large think about you.

One of the more positive things about growing older and maturing is that it becomes less and less important to you what other people think about you. You become more secure in who and what you are, and you are less likely to let yourself be defined by others.

When embarking on a spiritual journey in particular, it can be easy to let other people influence your thinking by discrediting your new ideas or letting the members of organized religion tell you that all this stuff comes from the devil and even thinking about it buys you a one-way ticket to hell.

Listening to all that noise coming from every direction can quickly shut down all forward progress. Learn to listen to your own inner voice.

The third and final thing on our list that we need to do can also help us deal with the first two: stop paying attention to what you perceive as your current reality. I know that may sound crazy, and in fact, one definition of insanity could be a detachment from reality, but not paying attention to reality in this sense doesn't mean going into an alternate reality while still living your current one.

It means changing the reality of what you don't want in your life into the reality of what you do want in your life.

A friend of Barb's told her recently that someone on the other side had sent her a message that said to ignore the grand illusion and make your own illusion grand. What a perfect sentiment to explain this concept.

In order for you to manifest all the good things you desire for your life, you have to stop giving attention to all the bad things. Your reality is what you make it.

The only thing we are ever in total control of is our emotions, so the inconvenient truth is that we choose to be happy all the time or miserable all the time, whether knowingly or not. Life is so much better when you choose happy.

To sum up this chapter, there are three things we need to change in order to move ahead spiritually by using the law of attraction are: get rid of the fear of change, get rid of caring about what other people think of you, and don't pay attention to your current reality.

Once we've done all that work, and it is work because it's not easy to alter long-held ideas and beliefs, we will be ready to start moving forward in our spiritual journeys with the ever-present help of our guides.

6

I'm Forever Blowing Bubbles

There are times when Jasper gets so exasperated with me being a dumb human that he does something to show his displeasure. During a recent session with Barb, we got sidetracked talking about a mutual friend who was having some problems, and an hour passed before we even realized it.

Barb always records our sessions on her phone and sends them to me via email because, at my advanced age, it's difficult to remember everything we talk about and learn each time.

At the end of this particular session, Barb picked up her phone to forward me the recording and noticed that the phone had been shut off—even though I saw her turn it on at the beginning of the hour. That meant there was no hard copy of the day's discussion. Disaster!

As a result, I had to hurry home and quickly write down everything I could remember about what we had learned. It was important information, and in fact, it was the subject of this chapter. I sent my transcript to Barb, and she tried to fill in the gaps, but I still didn't have a clear understanding of everything we had talked about.

The next day, I got an email from Barb with the subject title: "Listen to this—Jasper was our guide."

It turns out that Jasper had turned off Barb's phone recorder because he was displeased that we weren't focused on what he was trying to tell us. And, yes, they can do that from the other side because they are basically an advanced form of energy over there, so they can mess with our electronics over here. A lot of people have had departed loved ones make the lights flicker or the phone ring, so it's not uncommon.

Anyway, he was feeling guilty for pulling his little prank, so he decided to pop into a session Barb was having with another client and show the two of them what he had intended to show Barb and me before our meeting went off track.

More than a few times, Barb has asked me how I put up with Jasper, but I know he's only acting the way I asked him to before I incarnated this time. I knew I would need him to be over the top or I would have ignored him. As much as I wish I could get my hands on him and smack him sometimes, I know he is what he is for my benefit.

It's the same with all our soul guides. They are what we need and want them to be. I just didn't realize that when I asked for Jasper to be the colorful personality that he is, he would be able to inflict himself on other people. To the few who have experienced him, I apologize.

But back to the subject at hand. As I was listening to the recording of the session between Barb and her client being guided on a train trip to the other side by Jasper, I got a clear picture of the proceedings. For his guest appearance, Jasper chose to look like Ringo Starr when he was playing the conductor on *Thomas the Tank Engine*.

Let me tell you a little about the excursion he took them on, and then we can discuss what they experienced when they got to their destination.

Jasper had them picture themselves boarding an old-fashioned train that was red for no particular reason other than Jasper likes red. The train left the station and went through what looked to me like a kaleidoscope where the colors were bright and always changing.

After a minute or two, the train arrived at another station that Barb described as looking like it was out of a painting by an Impressionist like Van Gogh. To me, it looked like the artwork from Dr. Seuss's *The Lorax*. The trees resembled cotton candy, and the colors were very vivid but not exactly earthlike. The trees were blue, the grass was yellow, and the sky was kind of turquoise.

Jasper had them get off the train, and he attached them to him with silver tethers so they wouldn't get lost. As they walked over the top of a little hill, a vast field came into view. It was filled with clear domed structures that were about the size of a person stretching away as far as the eye could see. To Barb, it looked like a giant field covered in bubbles.

The bubbles were clear, and they appeared to be empty, but they contained massive amounts of the vibrational energy of every person incarnated on the earth plane. As it turns out, they are the containers on the other side where we store a part of us that we leave behind when we come here to live a life.

When we are planning for our incarnation, our motto always is "Pack light" because we only bring the parts of our energy we're going to need to cope with the scenarios we've chosen for ourselves.

I've written before that we only bring about 10 percent of our intellect with us from the other side, with many politicians bringing noticeably less, so the 90 percent we leave behind has to be stored somewhere, hence the billions of bubbles in this field.

We leave the parts of our personality we won't be using in our guides, but we leave our pure vibrational energy in the bubbles.

Each person has their own private bubble that even our spirit guides can't access. We are the only ones with the code to the door, and even we have to attain a fairly high vibrational level to get in when we're incarnated, which is another reason for focusing on improving our connection to our guides and, through them, the other side.

Our positive thoughts can connect us to our energy reserves on the other side if we can direct them there. You might want to think of them as similar to the thought bubbles that contain the dialogue in many cartoons. We have that big bubble with our vibrational energy stored in it, but without the smaller bubbles coming from us and going there, we can't make a connection.

You may think all this sounds like it was taken from some weird comic book and is just about as believable. I get it. I almost deleted this entire chapter, but the guides said it was important information for those who would be able to grasp it.

In allowing us to see and know about this particular area of the other side, Jasper is teaching us another way to use the positive side of the law of attraction to aid us in our soul growth by using the energy reserves we store there to help us move toward our goals.

Consider the bubble field to be a reservoir of energy that you can tap into for feelings of emotional safety. It's the storage space for all the knowledge you left behind about being one with the universe, and it is bound together by unconditional love.

There is no negativity in your bubble—just calm, gentle unconditional love that you can use to help you deal with the unending barrage of negativity you face in your everyday earth life.

Everything you need and desire is in the bubble, and it can all be accessed by believing, allowing, and using positivity to bring it to you.

Like that chain of small bubbles that connects the cartoon character to his dialogue in the thought bubble, we are always connected to our bubbles by how we think about the things that are happening in our lives. We can use that connection just like a nurse uses an IV drip to infuse medication into a patient—only the fluid will be replaced by more positivity.

The clamp that regulates the flow of energy is simply belief. Nothing can disconnect you from the infusion other than you losing the belief that it is there and available.

You need to practice having an awareness of your bubble and knowing you have access to it. From that will come an expectation of change.

Once you begin to feel safe about accepting change for its own sake, you can always come back to your bubble for direction on how to best utilize your new emotions. It's like an earth life survival kit.

We put all our hopes, dreams, and desires in there before we incarnate, add to them by our thoughts while we're here, and then, by using the law of attraction, we can access them to manifest what we want.

We will never run out of desires, and that's the way it's supposed to be. If we are overly satisfied with the way things are, we might as well pack it in and go home. We should be happy in the feeling of never being satisfied.

Satisfaction and happiness bring inertia, and with too much of that, we won't be learning anything, so what's the point of staying?

To sort of wrap things up in this chapter, though there is a lot of new information here that will take some time to digest, remember that we are all individuals on our own unique journeys. We have charted our own spiritual growth at our own chosen pace.

Some people will see the bubbles as holding all their hopes and dreams, and they will embrace the idea of them and do everything they can to increase their access to their own personal one.

Others may see the bubbles as a safe space where it's possible to think about and imagine any life scenario without fear of judgment by themselves or others.

And, of course, other people will think it's just a bunch of New Age bull, and that's okay too.

The bubbles are a lot like the Room of Requirement at Hogwarts. If you really believe the place is there, and if you believe what you need is in there, you will be able to find it.

Our own personal bubble might be considered the last stop on the victory lap we all take when we transition back to the other side after an incarnation. We go through detox, healing, life review, karma list compounding, and the bragging room.

As the final piece of our total reintegration into our real lives, we enter our storage bubble to recharge our vibrational level and remind ourselves of the goals and dreams we have in mind for future incarnations.

At the very least, we can take comfort in knowing that there is a lot more to us and our lives than we can currently see or understand. The biggest, best, and brightest part of us is waiting at home, and we can access it by focusing on bringing more positivity into our lives.

Since we're already fantastic beings in our human forms, imagine how much more fantastic we could be by bringing even a little more of all that positive vibrational energy into our daily lives.

7
Waiting

In 1981, Tom Petty and the Heartbreakers released "The Waiting," which contains that famous line: "The waiting is the hardest part." As the old saying goes, truer words were never spoken.

Once you have a clear understanding of the law of attraction, that it is the universal truth that like attracts like, have decided to allow the other side to help you move in a more positive direction, and have submitted your work order to the universe for that to start happening, what do you do next?

You wait. You don't try to force the issue. You wait. And as someone who recently went through what I felt was an overly long waiting period for something I really wanted to happen, I can absolutely understand how the waiting is, indeed, the hardest part.

Before we actually get into what we can all do during our periods of waiting for the changes we've requested to start happening in our lives, we should talk about the three major areas of our earth lives that cause the vast majority of us the most concern.

Those three things, in no particular order, are money, relationships, and health concerns. Let's talk about money first because it seems to be the part of our lives that we can lose the most sleep over.

A very few people have a fear of having too much money because they think it would change their lives in ways they couldn't cope with and destroy important relationships they've spent a lifetime creating.

Not to minimize the concerns of that very small group of people, but most of the rest of us find it hard to comprehend how having a lot of money could possibly be a bad thing. Since the majority of us worry about never having enough money, let's concentrate on that.

The law of attraction tells us that the universe hears what we think about, and it wants to give us whatever that may be, so if our only thoughts about money are that we never have enough, we're never going to have enough because the universe is there to help us achieve our goals.

The goal it hears us thinking about most is never having enough money. That's what it thinks you want, and it will make sure you get it.

I know it's been said and written over and over again, but the only way to change your life is to change the way you look at the things that are bothering you and then change the way you think about them.

The reason this topic has been written about thousands of times by thousands of different people is that it's a fundamental truth, and it's also the first step in using the law of attraction as a change agent to direct you in a more positive direction.

So back to concerns about money.

You absolutely must stop thinking about money in a "negative-balance" type of way. And here is where another important point about letting the universe help you comes into play. If you keep thinking, *By the end of the month, I want a million dollars in the bank and a brand-new Mercedes in the driveway of my new expensive house,* it's just not going to happen unless you hit the lottery.

The law of attraction is always about baby steps. When we incarnate on this planet, our puny human minds, as Jasper always likes to remind us, are incapable of grasping large universal concepts and life changes without literally exploding, so it's always going to be progress by small, incremental steps.

Often times, Jasper will tell Barb and me something during a session that will enlighten us in a new way. I will say, "You told us that months ago."

He will say, "I told you, but you really weren't ready to hear and understand it."

Of course, that is always true. When he does that, it's his little way of testing the progress in expanding the thinking that Barb and I are doing, and by extension, our overall learning.

But I digress. The best way for us to use the law of attraction to our advantage is, once we've identified the scenario in our lives that we most want to change, to identify a goal and then take baby steps toward it.

It's not a huge goal, like the winning-the-lottery scenario from before; it's a smaller and more generalized goal. We set goals for ourselves our whole lives, beginning with wanting to pass tests in school, then wanting to get accepted at college, then wanting to graduate and find a job, buy a house, etc.

We may not even realize we are setting goals because we don't label them as such, but it's something we are used to doing.

In reality, you're never going to reach your goal anyway, but that's not a bad thing. Your goals are always going to be changing as you progress through life.

Even if you think of climbing Mount Everest as your goal, after you do that, your goal might change to flying into outer space in a commercial aircraft. After that, it might be to colonize Mars. Who knows? The only time your goals stop changing is when you decide you've done as much as you wanted to do in this life and you go home to start planning your next incarnation.

In relating this concept to money, the first thing you have to do is be realistic. As the old saying goes, when you find yourself in a hole, the first thing you need to do is quit digging. If you are having trouble paying the electric bill, but you are still buying that six-dollar latte every morning, you have to let some common sense come into play.

Even though it pains me to use another old saying because it smacks of the sin-and-punishment theme of organized religion, I will say that the lord helps those who help themselves because it's true.

There's a reason that sayings become old, and that is because they stand the test of time. In the last one, I would change the word *lord* to *universe* because they really are the same thing—just with the religious context removed.

Once you've gotten your financial house in as much order as possible, it's time to start changing your thoughts and feelings about money. Going back to our baby steps theme, you're going to start thinking something like, *This month, I will have enough money to pay the bills. Even if there isn't much left over, I will have enough to pay the bills.* Then believe it and wait for it to happen.

Since the theme of this chapter is waiting, let's talk a little about something else we can do while we wait: looking for and noticing signs that our guides on the other side are trying to give us to help us as we're changing our way of thinking.

In our human condition, we often choose to largely ignore their help—sometimes because we have trouble identifying it as help and sometimes because we don't believe and allow that it is real.

Maybe it's autumn, and something tells you that you should try on your winter coat—and you just happen to find a twenty-dollar bill in the pocket that will help cover some bills this month. Maybe you hear about someone needing computer help, pet sitting, or something else in your area of expertise that could help you earn a few extra bucks. I've written about this type of help from your guides before, so let me give another example.

A friend had a lot of money problems when she was younger and fell months behind in her car payments. The credit union that had financed the loan kept calling and finally said they were going to have to repossess her car. My friend felt totally defeated by chronic money problems at that point, and she told them to come take it. She couldn't fight it anymore.

After a brief silence on the other end of the line, the credit union offered to work with her and refinance. After she did, she was able to keep the car—with a much lower monthly payment that she could actually afford. If she had persisted in trying to fight to keep the car, she would undoubtedly have lost it, but in that moment of surrender, her guides were able to step in and give the lender an idea about how to make things work out.

I'm sure everybody out there has heard a similar story, and thought, *Wow, what a coincidence. How lucky was that?* As I'm always fond of saying, there are no coincidences—only our friends on the other side who are trying to help us.

Even though we all have lots of souls on the other side who are willing to do anything to help us accomplish everything we planned for ourselves before coming into this life, they cannot and will not just hand us everything on a silver platter. We have to put in the time and effort necessary to change the direction of our lives for the better.

You're going to have to put in some serious work and do a lot of self-examination and introspection before the self-improvement process can begin.

If you are happy with who you are and where you are in life, then there is no impetus to change. Then again, if you feel that way, I guess you wouldn't be reading this book in the first place. So, for those of us who are feeling the need for change, let's move on to the next biggest life issue people struggle with, and that is relationships: the lack of one or having one that is not working out.

For the lack of a relationship, the same rules exist that apply to money. If you are continually thinking about the person who has not come into your life in terms of "they're not here," they will never "be here" because the universe hears you repeating that phrase and is happy to make that happen for you.

You have to alter your thinking so that instead of bemoaning the absence of someone, you are always and only thinking that they are out there and they are coming.

As Michael Bublé sang, "You just haven't met them yet." Or you have met them, but the relationship hasn't progressed as you thought it would—yet. We're still talking about baby steps, and you have to give things time to evolve as they should. But since our emphasis in this chapter is on waiting, what do you do while you're waiting for "the one" to come into your life?

Well, Jasper hasn't had much to say on this particular topic because he gets bored to tears with what he considers to be human whining about nothing, but he is ready to make an appearance as Liza (with a Z) Minelli as she appeared in *Cabaret* to ask, "What good is sitting alone in your room? Come hear the music play." Actually, he makes a pretty good Liza—they have the same eyes and presurgerical nose.

Anyway, Jasper's theatrics aside, the baby steps to use on your way to the relationship you want are to practice being in that relationship before it even starts. If you don't have a special someone to meet for drinks after work, go with some friends. Try out feeling the emotion of what it would be like to have a significant other to meet. Act like you already have what you want.

There is always somebody or a group of somebodies around who are up for going to the movies or out to dinner. While you are doing that, you can flirt with the waiter or the bartender, or just say hello to the people around you at the theater or restaurant. You never know who you might meet.

The worst thing you can do is sit at home, stare out the window, and hope Prince Charming will ride up on his horse and whisk you away to a fairy-tale life. That is most likely never going to happen.

There is no harm in going out, being among people, and having a little fun. Soon, you'll be wanting to do that more and more just because it feels good, and feeling good about yourself will become your new normal.

Turning the law of attraction from negative to positive for yourself will make it that much easier to attract someone positive into your life.

The last of the big three life issues that can be dealt with by altering the polarity of the law of attraction for you personally is health.

I don't really mean disease states because that topic could fill a book of its own. I mean health in the sense of feeling as good as you can on a day-to-day basis and keeping your physical body in its most functional capacity.

I'm not going to talk about smoking or drug and alcohol addiction—those disease states are also worthy of their own books—but there is another addiction that can be overcome by using the law of attraction: an addiction to food.

I don't have to go on at length about the obesity epidemic in this country. All anyone has to do is look around to see how many people are affected by an addiction to food, specifically the wrong kinds of food.

So how can we use the law of attraction to help us lose weight? As with money and relationships, we have to start with baby steps and set goals that are attainable.

If your first thought about losing weight is, *I have to lose twenty-five, fifty, or one hundred pounds,* you're going to feel defeated the first time you step on the scale and have only lost a pound or two. All you will be able to think about is how far you have to go. Or even worse, you will think, *I can never lose all this weight.*

This is where you have to redirect your thinking. First and foremost, get rid of the word "only." You didn't only lose a pound—you lost a whole pound! That's great! It's a baby step in the right direction. Celebrate that and let it make you feel good about yourself. Once you start feeling good about the small steps forward, hold on to that feeling so you keep making those small steps.

Set goals by thinking, *For the next four or six hours, I will not eat any sweets,* and then don't. Congratulations! You just hit another baby-step goal! It will feel so good that you can make those hours turn into days in small, manageable chunks rather than a drastic all-or-nothing change.

Start setting other baby-step goals—*Today I will only drink water instead of the two-liter Coke I usually drink*—and then do it. You may backslide tomorrow, but you met your goal today, and it felt pretty damn good.

Losing weight is one of the hardest things to do on this planet because carrot sticks are never going to taste like Little Debbies. The only way it can be done is by playing mind games with yourself and using the positive side of the law of attraction.

If your thoughts about yourself tend to be along the lines of, "I'm so fat, I'm so fat," that's what the universe hears and wants to help you achieve. Change that negativity to a positive: "I will lose weight." Adjust your goals to make them more general in nature. Don't say you will lose fifty pounds. Keep it nonspecific and say you are going to lose weight.

After all, you gained the weight a pound at a time, so you have to lose it a pound at a time.

Weight has become a huge issue in America today, no pun intended, and is a major health concern due to the other diseases it contributes to, like high blood pressure, diabetes, and heart disease, but dealing with obesity is not just about losing weight. It's about feeling good in general.

If you don't feel good about yourself, it's going to make losing those pounds even more difficult.

Once again, we have to look to changing the polarity of the law of attraction from negative to positive. Too many people wake up in the morning and think, *I'm so tired. My knees/hips/joints/back hurt. I don't want to do what I have to do today, and I hate my life in general.* I think we all have those days—some more than others. I know I do.

So, going back to the law, if the universe hears you constantly saying, "My knees hurt," or, "I know today is going to be miserable," what is going to happen? You should know the answer by now. The universe will help you feel the pain in your knees and have a miserable day to boot. And guess what else? You should know what comes next by now too.

Using baby steps, you think, *My knees might hurt, but I can still get around, and after I get moving, they will hurt less. On top of that, I think I'm gonna have a pretty good day just to spite myself.* If you can force yourself to feel good about things and change the negative to positive, the positivity will start creating more positivity. Like being in a twelve-step program, you've got to take one day at a time. You have to start from where you are and not from where you want to end up. That is a truism for managing all three of the life issues we just talked about.

The common theme that runs through the "big three" life issues is that they belong to each of us individually. We have to own them, and then after that, we have to decide if and how we are going to deal with them. Are we going to feel like victims and wallow in our problems, or are we going to use our knowledge of the law of attraction to gain control over the issue, manage it, and move forward?

One of the new ideas that changed the way I see things was being told that we will never reach our goals because as we grow, learn, and evolve, so do our goals. I think all of us of a certain age can relate to that by thinking about how our tastes have changed as we matured.

When we were younger, maybe with children at home, McDonald's or Wendy's was a big treat. From there, as we aged a little, we moved on to TGI Fridays or Applebee's. Eventually, you get to a point where a really good steak house like Morton's or Ruth's Chris is the only thing that really appeals to you. See how that fixation on food can creep into our thoughts so easily?

There may also be some evolving on many issues involved here, but I think it's mostly about changing tastes and thinking about things you feel you deserve. This whole game of life is meant to enable us to move forward in every sense—and never be completely happy where we are.

All of our life experiences compound, almost on a daily basis, to give us the desire to keep resetting our goals and accomplish bigger and better things.

Jasper is telling me I've gone way off track in a chapter that's supposed to be about waiting for change, but everything I've written about is important.

Let me wrap this up by saying that after you make a conscious decision to use the law of attraction to change the direction of your life to a more positive one, waiting to see signs that the change is happening can be difficult.

It's a lot like waiting in the doctor's office when it's already thirty minutes past your appointment time. The old you—and me—would get increasingly agitated, fuss, fume, and fidget, maybe get up and pace around, and wonder if we're ever going to get in to see the doctor.

The new you—who has an understanding of the law of attraction and wants all the benefit of using its positive side—knows you will be seen by the doctor when the time comes, so you can use our wait to answer texts or play games on your phone.

You might even do something old school like read a magazine and maybe find some useful information in there instead of thinking you will never get to see the doctor because the universe will make that happen for you.

The secret to waiting, and this can apply to many aspects of life, is choosing your focus. With money, do you focus on your lack of it or on the thought that you have enough to pay the bills right now? With relationships, do you focus on not having a soul mate to have fun with or on having fun with your friends while you're waiting? With health issues, do you focus on having pain and discomfort or on feeling better?

Only you can choose the scenarios playing out around you that you will pay attention to. Only you can decide what really does and does not matter to you as you try to grow spiritually.

I would be remiss if I ended this chapter without giving you Jasper's suggestion for distracting yourself from the negativity in your life. He calls it the squirrel exercise.

To play the game, you have to pretend you're a dog being walked on a leash. When you start feeling the negativity creep in because what you want hasn't come along just yet, you say, "Squirrel" out loud and act like a dog does when he spies a squirrel while he's out walking.

The dog completely forgets about what he was looking at and goes charging off in another direction. Now, if you're at work or in a group of people, it probably isn't a good idea to randomly shout, "Squirrel!" In those situations, just think it to yourself.

Though Jasper and I both think it would be hilarious if people started shouting, "Squirrel!" in public places. We share the same preadolescent-boy sense of humor.

Finally, when you feel like you've been waiting in that office for the door to open and your name to be called for so long that the apple you were eating has turned brown, try any of these distractions to keep you away from negativity. The door will always eventually open. The catch, which cleverly leads us to the next chapter, is that there's always another door.

8

There's Always Another Door

There's always another door? Well, that just sounds depressing.

You mean, no matter how hard I work at changing my entire outlook on life from negative to positive while I'm sitting in that waiting room, when the door opens and I go through it, I enter another waiting room with another door? How can that be? Why bother trying to improve myself if I can't make any progress? What's the payoff for me if I just keep seeing another door?

Those are all legitimate questions, and if you can simmer down for a minute, I think our friends on the other side can supply some answers.

Remember how they told us that we never really reach our goals because they are always evolving just as we are? Didn't that sound depressing at the time? You—and I initially—said, "You mean to tell me that my reward for doing good work is more work?" Yes, gentle reader, that seems to be the state of things.

The problem with viewing your spiritual growth and advancement as equivalent to graduating from high school or college or winning a sports event is that you are viewing spirituality from your very human perspective.

In our earth lives, we've become accustomed to working hard to cross a finish line, crossing it, and then being done. It seems natural and normal to feel that way because that's our life experience, and the same holds true for most of the people around us.

It takes some rearranging of your thought processes to be able to understand that spiritual growth is limitless, and since there are no boundaries, there can never be an end point. We never get to a place where we can look back on everything we've accomplished and say, "That's it. I'm done."

The closest comparison to spiritual growth in this dimension might be acquiring knowledge for the sake of having knowledge. You graduate from high school (door), go to college and get your bachelor's degree (another door), get your master's degree (another door), and get your doctorate (another door).

You may become the foremost expert in whatever your field of study might be, but after going through all those doors, if you are truly wise, you will know that there is always more to be learned and more discoveries to be made.

I've already written about how you can consider your life in this dimension to be like a doctor's waiting room.

You've put in all the work of self-examination and soul-searching to determine where you are in life, and, more importantly, where you want to go. You've expressed your desires to the universe by using the law of attraction in a positive way, and the universe is working diligently behind the scenes to prepare everything for you.

But you're still going to have to spend some time in that waiting room while you come into alignment with your desires.

While you're waiting, you have to start to feel comfortable about the space you're in.

Going back to the waiting room, and we've all been there, you see basically two types of people. The first type are the ones who look like they are ready to jump out of their skins. They sigh, shift around in their seats, or pace around the room. They may even berate the receptionist and say, "Don't you realize how important my time is?"

The second type of person will sit quietly, text or play games on their phones, or read a magazine. Basically, they will enjoy having some time to relax and contemplate the fates and destinies.

Which type of person do you think you are? I freely admit that I used to be the first type, like a lot of us, but acting that way doesn't make that door open any faster than it's supposed to.

In fact, by manifesting so much negativity, it may even delay the door opening.

In recent years, I've become more like the second person, enjoying the time to sit and think in peace and being comfortable in the space I'm in.

Feeling comfortable in your own space, especially in your own skin, is one of the most important things we all have to learn before the universe is going to allow that next door to open and let us move on to another waiting room.

Actually, it's less the universe allowing the door to open than it is allowing ourselves to trust and believe that the door will open when we are ready to move on to the next challenge.

Even though the guides have described these life scenarios that we're living out as being equivalent to waiting rooms, they really could also be compared to the escape rooms that have become so popular in recent years.

An escape room, for those who don't know, is a place where you can go and pay someone to lock you in a room, and within an allotted amount of time, you have to find and interpret clues that will lead you to a key that will unlock the door, thus accomplishing the aforementioned escape.

It's sort of like a scavenger hunt, but it's all contained in one room.

Whether it makes more sense to you to call it a waiting room or an escape room, the things we want to accomplish while we're in there are exactly the same.

First, we want to feel comfortable with who we are because no matter how many doors we go through in a lifetime, we are the single constant that keeps moving on. In fact, even though we may not realize it at the time, we actually choose what we want to take with us into the next room, which is the next life scenario we will be living out.

We may pass through dozens of doors in each lifetime, and we may be in some waiting rooms for only a brief time, or a much longer time, but each room is there for us to work on our spiritual selves.

Whatever tools we need to do that work will come from our own life experiences and from the help the guides are always trying to give us.

No matter how much time we spend in each room, our primary job there is to find and figure out what we want to take with us through the next door and into the next room. We have to gather up as many positives as we can and leave as many negatives behind us as possible.

We're fortunate in that we can make a conscious decision that we've had enough of certain negatives in our lives. We decide we're just not going to carry them forward with us into the next room.

Those negatives can include anything and everything from old thought processes to toxic people in your life. Being ready to go through that next door when it opens is a wonderful opportunity for change because once the old door closes behind you, it stays closed.

Jasper just showed up looking like Gene Wilder from *Young Frankenstein*. He wants us to remember that great scene where Dr. Frankenstein asks Igor and Inga to lock him in a room with the monster and not open the door no matter what he says or how much he begs. Of course, within minutes, he's pleading with them to open the door, and the usual Mel Brooks hilarity ensues. Great movie.

The point Jasper is trying to make is that at one time or another, we've all been or will be Dr. Frankenstein pleading for the door that just closed to open and let us go back through to our old life because we're afraid of the monster in the new room. That isn't going to happen, so like Dr. F., we have to calm down and look for the good in our new life scenario.

I'm reminded of a terrific children's book featuring the beloved Sesame Street character, Grover.

In *The Monster at the End of this Book*, Grover reads on the first page that there is a monster at the end of the book, so he does everything he can to keep the reader from turning pages. He builds a brick wall, nails pages together, and tries to tie everything up with rope.

Of course, the reader keeps turning pages, and in the end, the monster turns out to be an embarrassed Grover.

These types of books are just another example of the many ways the other side uses entertainment in all its forms to teach us life lessons—if we can just learn to see them.

We are always afraid of moving forward, and we do everything we can think of not to have to, but in the end, the fear is brought on by us and our subconscious not wanting to change or learn anything new. We are all the monster at the end of our own books.

But I digress. Time only moves forward in this dimension—never backward. If you're really determined to swim against the tide, you may be able to tread water for a while and make things stagnate in your life, but the current of time will eventually move you forward—whether you want to go or not.

Do you move forward gladly or move forward in such an exhausted state from trying to swim upstream that you can't appreciate and enjoy the journey.

In one of my earlier books, I talked about all the emotional baggage I was choosing to carry along with me in my life's journey this time. I had enough accumulated garbage from this lifetime and some of my past lives that Jasper showed me it actually filled a good-sized freight train. I know that my situation was not unique or special and that millions of people are pulling the same burdens with them without even realizing it.

After a lot of spiritual work over the last few years, and with a lot of guidance from Jasper, I've managed to let a lot of it go.

By "it," I mean a significant amount of fear, anger, and guilt, and also a number of people, family members included, who were contributing nothing but toxicity to my life. I have that big freight train pulling many boxcars whittled down to a few suitcases, even though Jasper says they are more like steamer trunks.

Whatever the case, I've come a long way from where I started.

The important message here is that at the beginning of our spiritual journeys in each lifetime, the doors you have to go through between each scenario are big enough for those boxcars to also fit through, but as you learn to deal with your issues and make progress, each succeeding door gets smaller. Eventually the doors will only fit you—and all the positivity you carry inside.

As you grow spiritually, you will be leaving behind a lot of baggage, either consciously or unconsciously, so that with each new room, each new life scenario, more and more is left behind. That doesn't mean many of us won't try to drag something through the door that isn't going to fit. We're only human after all, and we're natural-born hoarders of things we should be happily getting rid of.

If what we're holding onto—old feelings, old programs, anger, fear, guilt, or relationships—won't fit through the door into the next room, we have to choose between progressing on our journey and being stuck in the room we're in.

If you're reading this book, I'm assuming you are progressing nicely in the journey to grow your soul, but if you happen to be stuck and just can't force yourself through that next door, it's not a catastrophe. It only means that you're going to be dealing with that baggage you can't leave behind in your next life.

Wouldn't it be better to deal with it now and start with a clean slate next time around? That's what I'm trying to do now that I've been given the knowledge of how this all works.

If you've read anything else I've written, you're probably aware that Jasper's all-time favorite movie is *The Wizard of Oz*, the 1939 version starring Judy Garland, of course.

He likes it for a number of reasons—and not just for the pretty colors. He likes to draw analogies from the movie to teach Barb and me about universal principles, like us always being in control of our own destinies with help from our guides, as Dorothy was with help from the ruby slippers.

Recently, for the teaching purposes of this book, he's been showing us scenes from *Alice in Wonderland*, especially the part where Alice finds a vial with a tag that says, "Drink me."

After Alice drinks whatever potion is in the vial, she shrinks enough to fit through a small door and continue on her journey.

He says that passing through the door between our life scenarios works exactly the same way. If we would only listen when our guides say, "Drink this," whether we want to or not, it would make it much easier to fit through the next door.

Talking about doors and using them as metaphors to signify opening yourself to new ideas makes a lot of sense to me personally, so I'm glad the other side has decided to use it as a teaching tool.

Doors can be considered to be both barriers and openings to progress, but you have to remember that the door doesn't decide which one it will be—you do.

You have to want the door to be an exit or to keep you in. It's not the door's fault if it doesn't open like you think it should. You are the only one who can open your own doors, but that work can be made easier with help from the other side.

Once you've progressed far enough in your spiritual journey, you will come to realize that, just like goals, the number of doors can be infinite.

As you gain more insight and knowledge, the doors you have access to keep increasing in number. Jasper recently showed Barb and me a lot of doors without steps leading to them. He said we have a lot more to learn before we get to open those doors; thankfully, he's willing to teach us what we need to know to get there.

The biggest takeaway from this chapter has to be remembering that the only constant in all of this is you. You are the one going through every new door, and it's your choice who and what you take with you.

As Jasper has told me, he may look like Ethel Merman in one room, and Ginger Rogers in the next, but he's always Jasper at the heart of his craziness. Sometimes I think some of those steamer trunks he accuses me of dragging along are filled with his many costumes and not my emotional baggage. It would be just like him to use me as his roadie!

9

Go Bait and Switch Yourself

Jasper and the other guides are always telling Barb and me about different ways to look at the same scenarios. They hope giving us a number of options will help us understand things. If one of them makes sense, something will click in our puny human minds.

I think it is important to share any and all of those tricks they have been giving us with you, gentle reader. If one explanation doesn't resonate with you or make a lot of sense, perhaps one with different wording will. I promise not to roll my eyes like Jasper does when I don't get it the first time.

Everyone hears what they want and need to hear. If your vibrational level doesn't match the concept you're trying to understand, it doesn't mean you're stupid or unable to learn, it just means you have some more spiritual growth to accomplish before you can have a complete understanding of the subject at hand.

I certainly feel like I am learning new things all the time—even things I thought I already understood. If I live to be one hundred, I expect to be learning new things until the day I transition.

The limitless size of the universe is beyond human comprehension, and when we're incarnated on this planet, our intellect is limited, but that doesn't mean we can't learn as much as possible under the circumstances.

As an added bonus, the more we're able to learn about our spirituality in this life means the less time we'll have to spend relearning things in our subsequent lives.

In the last chapter, I compared our many life scenarios to waiting rooms, but they might be more aptly equated with classrooms.

While we are, indeed, waiting for the door to open to our next life scenario all the time, we are accomplishing learning and soul growth by living out the lessons in our current situations. If we're not learning, we can become complacent about even wanting to make progress.

As humans, we need some drama and excitement in our everyday lives to keep up our desire to move forward. If we're completely happy and satisfied with our lives, feel we've accomplished whatever it was we came here to do, or are demoralized to the point of not caring, then learning has stopped—and we might as well pack it in and go home.

We need to keep our anticipation of what's coming next alive and growing and not let fear of change stop our forward progress.

One of the questions that is frequently asked by people starting on a new spiritual journey is one that I used to wonder about myself: "I know I want to change my life, but I don't have a clear picture of where I want to go. If I'm not really 100 percent sure what I need or want, how do I know what help to ask for?"

That is a really excellent question, and it's also a great starting place. It's like that old proverb about a journey of a thousand miles starting with the first step. If you're not sure what direction to go, how do you point your feet in the right direction?

Here is where we go back to the trusting and allowing that we discussed previously. We have to trust that our spirit guides are on the other side giving us direction, even if we don't hear their voices plainly in our heads, and we have to allow ourselves to believe they are pointing us in the direction we planned for ourselves to take before we incarnated.

The best course of action if you're unsure about what direction to take or what specific question will give you that information is to ask your guides to bring a scenario into your life that will provide the information and learning that you need.

Let's say you are thinking about moving to another city to take a new job, but you're unsure about making the move. Ask your guides for some clarification and manifestations about what you should do.

Within a short period of time, you will start hearing about the place you're thinking about moving more and more. You'll hear about it in either a positive or negative way in talking with friends, in overheard conversations, on the news, and on the internet—anywhere and everywhere.

If what you're hearing is mostly positive, then it should be a good move. If what you're hearing is mostly negative, then you should probably focus your job search elsewhere.

If your concerns are more about wealth and material things, don't ask directly to win the lottery. It will probably never happen, and if it should happen, it's doubtful you could hold on to the money.

We've seen that scenario play out so many times with big lottery winners being broke after a few years because they didn't ask to have the other side show them what it would feel like to be rich and then take the time to develop those emotions.

Narrow it down and take baby steps to get where you want to be. If you want a new Mercedes, ask for scenarios in your life that will teach you how to get to the point where you can afford that expensive new car.

Telling the universe, "Give me this now!" is never going to work.

First, we already discussed the time issue, so you need to remember that *now* on the other side might be tomorrow or ten years down the road. They're just not good with time, and you have to be in a place spiritually where you are ready to accept what they send.

Second, I'm going to assume that if you're reading this book, you're old enough to know that hardly anything of value is just handed to you. You have to wait for and earn what you want. Most importantly, you have to listen for the other side to tell you what you want and need to hear.

It's very easy to ignore all the signs the other side is sending your way. I know a few years ago, before my wake-up call, I was looking at moving and changing jobs, so I went to the city I was considering and job shadowed at the prospective new work place. Even though everything I was seeing and hearing told me I wouldn't like it, I moved and took the job. I lasted for about a year before I was looking to get out.

I could have saved myself and my family a lot of grief if I had only trusted my gut feelings, but I thought I knew better.

Even before I had a face and a name for Jasper, he was still there screaming in my ear and trying to guide me in the right direction. Of course, I let my Pennsylvania Dutch stubbornness be my guide most of the time back then, but even so, I knew inside me that it was a bad idea—and I still did it.

No detour off the yellow brick road on the way to our hopes and dreams is ever a bad thing. That's the moral of the story. There is always something to learn, and even though I didn't know about spirit guides at the time, I knew about intuition. I hadn't listened to mine.

Since they are the same thing, if you listen to your intuition, you are hearing the voice of your spirit guide.

In a spiritual sense, to get anything of real value, and more importantly, to be able to hold on to it, you have to ask the guides to give you scenarios in your life that will let you practice what it will feel like once you reach a particular goal.

Since we're on the subject of money, try thinking about what your emotions would be if you were wealthy. How would having a lot of money change you, if at all? How would the people around you change? Are you holding on to a fear that if you got rich and moved forward with your life, the people who you love might not move forward with you, and you would lose them?

I know it might sound funny to those of us who don't have a lot of money that some might be afraid of that, but the changes it can bring are an unknown that can cause a lot of anxiety. Back in the eighties, Cyndi Lauper sang "Money Changes Everything," and she was right. People who were your friends suddenly aren't, and people who weren't your friends suddenly are, and they all have their own agendas.

In order to prepare yourself for being wealthy, if that is your goal, you have to ask the guides to show you scenarios that are going to replace those fears and anxieties with a feeling of excitement about having money, or finding that special someone, or whatever it is you want.

We know moving ahead spiritually causes a change in our vibrational level, so ask your guides to let you feel what that increase would feel like. By doing that, you can speed the change in your current reality to the new reality you want to see. Your goal is never going to come to you—you have to keep moving toward your goal.

The funny thing about goals is, as you progress in your journey, not only do they keep moving, they can actually change into something completely different from what you originally had in mind.

By the time you get to the point where you can finally afford that new Mercedes, you may feel it better to keep your old Toyota and put that extra money in the bank. The expensive car that seemed so important way back when is no longer a priority, but in the striving for it, you learned how to make yourself financially successful enough to afford any car you want.

It now becomes a question of knowing that having that thing you wanted so badly doesn't make you feel happy and better about yourself, just having the feeling of knowing you can have it but don't really need it makes you feel happy and better about yourself.

To finally get to the point of the title of this chapter, the goals we set for ourselves are like the proverbial carrot on a stick that is placed in front of the donkey to get him to move forward.

It's the old bait and switch used by disreputable retailers for years. They lure customers into the store by advertising something at a ridiculously low price, and once they have you hooked, they talk you into buying something more expensive by telling you it's a better deal because the thing that was advertised is cheap but of low quality.

We do the same things to ourselves by setting a goal of being able to afford something expensive and then working and striving to be able to do that. You think about how great it will feel to possess that certain thing and how your life will be complete once you have it.

Over the course of the time it takes to get to your goal, you may find your feelings change, and once you get to where you thought you wanted to be, you want to keep moving on to something else.

In other words, once you get to where you can afford the Mercedes, you may want a Lamborghini. And once you can get the Lamborghini, you may decide you want a private jet, and after that, who knows?

Since you learned the lessons of acquiring and keeping wealth on your way to reaching the goal of being able to buy an expensive car, you can keep on using that knowledge to get yourself to a place where you can afford that jet.

In all likelihood, when you get to where you can buy an airplane, you may or may not buy it, but now that you've figured out how this law of attraction stuff works, especially when you are listening to your guides and letting them help you, you may reset your goals to being able to buy a yacht, go to outer space, or do something completely different than acquiring material things.

We will never be innately satisfied with where we are at any stage of our lives, and spiritually speaking, that is not a bad thing.

On this journey, we have to get excited about not feeling completely happy. Being in a state of bliss can cause spiritual inertia, which makes you want to remain where you are. Being too happy can lead to a state of spiritual smugness, and that won't do anything to help expand the universe.

Long periods of being too happy leads to boredom and the desire to stay where we are and stop moving forward. We have to give ourselves permission to not be satisfied and to hunger for more.

If you can incorporate getting more excited about change, and more importantly, what that change can bring into your life on a daily basis, then the time you have to worry about fear and what other people will think about you becomes less and less.

Once the fear of change and the worrying about what other people will think about you have been reduced to manageable levels, emotionally investing in your current reality can also be minimized. You will then have all that energy you used to expend on those three time wasters at your disposal to help you focus on your new reality, the one you have been envisioning for yourself.

Here again, use the old bait-and-switch technique to refocus your attention from your current reality and everything that people around you are saying onto what your guides are trying to tell you.

In Jasper's "squirrel" game, he says to think of yourself as a dog out walking through a park. He also says the dogs are a lot smarter than humans when it comes to emotions—and that we could learn a lot about unconditional love by observing them.

Be that as it may, picture the dog walking along when he suddenly spots a squirrel. He will stop focusing on whatever he was thinking about and go charging off in the direction of the squirrel, which has probably already gone up a tree.

That's how easy it can be to redirect your thoughts in an entirely new direction. If you feel you're getting bogged down in your present reality, pretend your new reality is a squirrel, focus completely on it, and go charging after it like our canine friend.

Challenge the idea that the only path forward is the one you are currently on.

Your guides can help you go in any direction you desire, but you have to let them know which way you want to go. You do that by focusing your attention on what you desire, be it money, a relationship, or anything else.

They can control the rudder on the boat that represents your life, but they will steer only toward what you are looking at and concentrating on. If you're having trouble seeing exactly where you want to go, ask your guides to help you. That's why they are called "guides." They know your entire life plan and can help you go in the direction you mapped out for yourself—even if it's unclear to you.

There are a few caveats here. The way forward is not always going to be smooth sailing. We are here to learn, after all, and the way we do that is by experiencing life scenarios that involve grief and emotional turmoil. We can only get that kind of direct learning by living in the negative atmosphere of earth, so that's why we come here.

The time it takes to negotiate the rough water and get back to smooth sailing is variable, and it depends a great deal on how well you are learning whatever lesson you have chosen for yourself.

Caveats aside, the point of this chapter is to realize that goals are a great thing to have, and they are absolutely essential to moving forward spiritually. They are also illusions, like reality itself, because once you get close to obtaining them, they change into something else, and another goal replaces the one you were pursuing.

Don't be depressed when that happens! It's the way the whole thing is supposed to work. Instead, go with the flow, and as we used to say back in the day, "Don't fight the feelin'."

At times, it's going to seem like you've been all dressed up and ready to go to the prom for a very long time. So long, in fact, that your corsage is wilting.

Again, the time you spend waiting for that big change to come is almost entirely up to you. It can take a lot of time to deal with the emotional baggage you are carrying with you, but until you do, forward progress will be slow.

For most of us, the trip will be baby steps a great deal of the time, but it's the journey, not the destination that is important, and it takes as long as it takes.

10

Bad Words Revisited

When we think about "bad words," the usual four-letter ones come to mind.

Those aren't the ones I want to focus on for this discussion. The words I want to talk about aren't swear words at all; they are everyday words that have taken on a negative connotation over the years, and those words are *selfish* and *entitled*.

Is there anybody alive who doesn't have childhood memories of their parents berating them for being selfish? Or kids accusing each other of being selfish at school or on the playground? Or buddies telling you not to be selfish and "bogart the j" in college? I think I really dated myself with that last one!

For our entire lives, we've been told by the world at large that being selfish is a bad thing.

It's still a bad thing when applied to large life issues like feeding and sheltering the homeless or taking care of the elderly, but when it comes to spirituality and personal growth, we really need to practice being selfish.

Before we can begin to move forward in our spiritual journey, we need to bring the focus of our lives back to ourselves. It can be an extremely difficult thing to do when we've been told all our lives not to do just that.

The textbook definition of selfishness from Wikipedia is "being concerned excessively or exclusively, for one's own advantage, pleasure, or welfare, regardless of others." It casts selfishness in a mostly negative light, but in our spiritual journeys, especially in the beginning stages, we're going to have to go there.

In order to increase our self-esteem, self-worth, and self-empowerment, we must become, at least for a while, concerned exclusively with our own spiritual welfare, regardless of what other people might think.

I've written before about my relationship with my mother when I was a child. I would characterize her as a self-esteem vampire, able to suck the joy out of any accomplishment of mine, big or small.

Those feelings of never being quite good enough continued into my adult years, and I kept allowing it to happen. My early programming, put in place by her, of course, would just keep running over and over, telling me it was wrong to feel good about myself for any achievement in my life.

It took many years and a lot of soul-searching to finally be able smash that old program and replace it with a Stuart Smalley-type affirmation from *Saturday Night Live*. You know the one where Al Franken looks into a mirror and says, "I'm good enough, I'm smart enough, and, darn it, people like me." Only you can replace that self-love that you were trained not to feel.

Even more important than self-esteem and self-empowerment is the one thing that has to come first and that they both depend on: unconditional self-love.

It's the same unconditional love that comes from source, but we have a hard time feeling it here on earth. We can't possibly feel the unconditional love that the universe has for us if we can't feel it for ourselves first.

Luckily, we have a direct link to all that unconditional love in the form of our guides. They dwell in a place of unconditional love, they have nothing but unconditional love for us, and if we can open up fully to them, they can assist in letting it flow into our lives.

Unconditional love means just what it says: love without conditions attached. Any conditions. Your subconscious is filled with things you think about yourself, mostly consisting of words about you that were put there by the people around you since the day you were born. And with the atmosphere of the earth plane being what it is, a lot of those words are negative.

Stupid, stubborn, selfish—and those a just a few that begin with the letter S. You've got a whole alphabet of crappy words about yourself that, just like your mother-in-law after a two-week visit, have got to go.

You can examine each one separately by thinking, *Am I stupid?* Give that one the boot and say, "No, I'm not!" If you're feeling a little stronger, you can tell your subconscious that you will no longer be putting conditions on your love for yourself, so it can open the pod bay doors and eject that stuff from the spaceship.

A problem can arise when your subconscious decides to be like the computer HAL from *2001: A Space Odyssey* and refuse to open the pod bay doors because it doesn't want to jettison an old functioning program until it has something better to take its place.

That is why it will take some time before you start feeling self-empowered by unconditional love.

However, once you get to a certain level, your subconscious will begin to cooperate and let go of that old programming. The level is different for everyone, and it depends on how lacking you are in self-love to begin with, but the theme of the other side is always baby steps, so don't be discouraged if it seems like you are taking two steps forward and three steps back.

Once you have strengthened your unconditional love for yourself, it makes it easier for the unconditional love of the universe to resonate with you and in you. Going into an extremely selfish mode for a while—until you can sort out your feelings for and about yourself—is not a bad thing spiritually.

It can, however, turn into a bad thing if you stay that way too long. That's when the final part of the definition of the word, "regardless of others," can come into play.

This is another one of those situations where you can let your guides do their jobs and direct you back to a place where you can hold onto your self-esteem and unconditional love of self and share that love with the important people in your life.

Another word that has developed an increasingly bad connotation in the last few years is *entitled.*

The Oxford Dictionary definition of *entitled* is that you believe yourself to be inherently deserving of privilege and/ or demanding and pretentious. I think it is the last part of the definition people think of when referring to the generation known as Millennials (those born between 1980 and 2000). All I can say in their defense is that they are living their lives the way their parents taught them to.

Putting people who camp out on the sidewalk overnight to get the latest version of an iPhone aside, spiritually, we need to modify the definition of entitled to be: I want it, I deserve it, and I expect it to happen.

By completely believing those things, we can develop a lot of self-confidence and self-esteem, which will help move us forward in our journeys. Once we truly understand that we are directly connected to the universe, our thoughts and dreams can be limitless.

By making "I want it, I deserve it, and I expect it to happen" a mantra for spiritual growth instead of applying only to material things, we can come to understand that we are entitled, just because we are alive at this time on this planet, and for no other reason, to feel free and deserving of whatever we want.

Feeling entitled to be or do whatever you want is vital to moving forward on your journey. After you've done the spiritual work to increase your self-esteem, a feeling of entitlement can give you a level of self-confidence that you've never experienced before. You're going to feel like you can have it all, and the only one who can tell you can't have it is you. If you think small, you feel small—so think big!

Your guides will be there to provide some balance, but let them know you now feel like you are entitled to see the best life scenarios available to you, so bring 'em on!

I'm not talking about what we call "spoiled brats"—more negative words that may be buried in our subconscious.

I think we've all experienced watching children ripping open Christmas present after Christmas present, barely looking at them, and then crying when all of them were opened because there were no more. That type of behavior comes about by only focusing on material things. When we set our sights on bringing more spirituality into our lives, it's perfectly okay to want more and more packages to open.

We were all taught to think that combination of entitlement and selfishness was a particularly odious type of behavior, but in our new way of thinking about those two "bad words," we have to learn to adopt a new spirit and say, "Okay, I've seen this. What's next?"

We have to want an experience-filled life. We have to be excited about changing our reality into a new and better one. Only by constantly asking, "What's next?" can we make that happen and expand the universe at the same time.

The Root of All Fear

I've written a lot about fear because—in the final analysis—fear is why we're here. Wouldn't that be a great advertising slogan for a Halloween haunted house? It's for sale if anyone is interested, but all kidding aside, it's a fundamental truth.

When we're at home on the other side and living our real lives—surrounded by unconditional love and connected to everyone and everything in the universe—fear doesn't exist. We intellectually understand that there is an emotion on the earth plane named "fear," but it's impossible to know what it actually feels like at home.

It's like telling a teenager to get up off the couch and walk to the TV to change the channel. They may get the concept, but they have never and will never have to actually do it, so it's just an odd little piece of trivia to them, and another reason for sighs and eye rolls.

If they really want to see and understand what that type of channel changing (and when I was young, it was a choice of three whole channels) was about, there is probably a YouTube video that shows how it was done, but it still wouldn't give them the experience of performing the real thing.

The same holds true for all of us when we're at home. We can view other people experiencing fear by accessing the records of all past lives that are kept over there, including our own.

Unlike our proverbial teenager who will never have to walk to a TV set to change a channel or adjust the volume, we can experience fear up close and in person by simply incarnating for a life here on earth, the fear capital of the universe.

The guides tell us that fear was first introduced on earth as a defense mechanism, providing humans with the old fight-or-flight reaction needed to avoid being eaten by giant bears or saber-toothed tigers. But fear has persisted long after those types of dangerous situations have disappeared, and it has morphed and evolved along with humans until today.

Fear has become a device used by religious and political leaders as a control mechanism and by your own subconscious as an internal way of slowing or stopping the changes that bring about spiritual advancement.

The subconscious mind is a complicated subject that has always been somewhat confusing for me. Why would a piece of our own minds work to keep us from growing spiritually when that is what we came here to do? It doesn't seem to make any sense, so let's backtrack a little and see if we can gain some perspective.

The subconscious mind in the world of psychology, as defined by Wikipedia, is simply that part of your consciousness that is not currently in focal awareness. In other words, since you can only be aware of so much information and knowledge at one time, everything else you know is stored in your subconscious.

In New Age thinking—and in the information I have been receiving from my friends on the other side—the subconscious is much, much more than that.

Your subconscious is the repository for all your memories, whether you perceive them to be good or bad, and it also acts as one of our connections to source and all the unconditional love on the other side.

By definition, unconditional doesn't judge things to be good or bad. It mostly wants things to flow smoothly, even if the direction you're taking isn't the one you planned for yourself. That connection, vital to our spiritual well-being though it may be, can sometimes cause us problems when we try to change our old programs.

The subconscious wants to do what works and what has worked for you in your life up to this point. Because it is part of the unconditional, it doesn't make judgments about whether what you have done in the past has been good or bad for you. It only wants to keep you on a steady path until it sees a new and steadier path available.

It doesn't care which way you are going, but until the idea for a different direction is solid and your subconscious knows you have no doubt about the new way forward being the right direction, it will do whatever it takes to mess with your mind and prevent you from changing.

It does not like change, and an incomplete or unformed thought about a new direction is not enough for the subconscious to want to move toward it.

That brings us to the fear part.

In my own life, once I identified that my fear of change was coming from inside me, from my own subconscious, I started to try to think of ways I could fight it.

I went back to my Saturday-morning cartoon days and thought about *Scooby Doo*. The kids in the gang were always investigating a haunting at the old mill, an abandoned amusement park, or someplace similar. It usually turned out that the haunter was the owner of the property dressed as a ghost or a yeti trying to collect on insurance or some other scam.

When the monster was captured, Shaggy or one of the others would pull the head off of his costume for the big reveal, whereupon the villain of the piece would say, "And I would have gotten away with it if it weren't for you kids."

I started picturing my subconscious as a guy in a bad ghost costume who was trying to scare me until I pulled the head of his costume off, punched him in the face, and told him to stop it.

Of course, he looked a lot like me because he is me. Sometimes I hesitated with the punch out of concern for hurting myself in some way. But, believe me, you're a lot tougher than you think you are. If you think it will help, punch away.

That method only worked for me about 50 percent of the time, but I'm happy to report that I've learned a new way to deal with my subconscious—and we can all use it in our own lives.

First, after a lot of thinking about it, I came to the realization that my subconscious wasn't there to punish me or hold me back. It was only trying to protect me by maintaining the status quo. Until I was able to use the law of attraction to focus on new goals—and believe in the new goals before I actually saw them—my subconscious just wanted to stay put.

By not encouraging you to run off in a new direction before you firmly believe your new path will lead you to what you really want, the subconscious can give you time to play in the emotions of having what you want. If your goal is to be wealthy, then you have to practice what you think it will feel like to be rich.

What do you believe it will be like? Will it bring you happiness, security, or freedom from any number of things? If you've never had a lot of money, you can't really know what it feels like, but you can practice what you think it will feel like.

By holding you back until you have a full understanding of what your goal consists of, and what your emotions will be once you attain it, your subconscious can provide clarity about what it will take to get you where you want to go.

You have to put yourself into a mode of absolute belief in what you want being available to you before the subconscious is going to stop trying to hold you back. You have to stop being afraid of change. You have to stop asking what, where, and when because that only puts conditions on your forward movement.

Most importantly, you have to trust and allow that the change can happen. Only by doing those things can you make your subconscious loosen its death grip on your old programming.

Holding on to even a small piece of your fear of change serves only one purpose, and it's one I've experienced myself. If you keep a little bit of that old negativity tucked away somewhere, it is going to hold you back. When what you want doesn't happen right away, you can say to yourself, "See? I knew it wouldn't work out."

When I used to say things like that to myself, I suppose it gave me some sort of sick satisfaction about being right—even when being right meant I had failed. But as the old saying goes, would you rather be right or happy?

You can't move forward if you keep sabotaging yourself in this way. You're playing right into the will of your subconscious to maintain the status quo. You have to be tired enough of dwelling in negativity to want moving out of it above all things. And you must develop at least the beginning of understanding what your emotions will be when you get to where you want to go.

In what I think is a really neat analogy, the other side says that the subconscious swells in the reality of whatever you're paying attention to. That means if you only concentrate on what you don't want, your subconscious grows to fill up that space so it is even harder to pull it out of that hole and make it move forward. You're playing right into the "no-change" policy that your subconscious loves to live by.

I know I've spent a lot of time making your subconscious sound like the bad guy for obstructing your desire to change and grow spiritually, but it is not acting the way it does out of any kind of malice. It just wants to keep you safe, and it thinks the best way to do that is by locking you in your room and never letting you come out.

The magic key that can open that locked door is having a desire for change, having an ultimate goal in mind, and then believing you can reach that goal before you actually see it. That is the theme of this entire book: believing without seeing.

Before any meaningful change can begin, you have to get yourself into a mode of complete belief. You can't expect the universe to show you anything different until you can totally believe there is something different to see. If you insist on constantly looking at crap, then the universe is going to keep showing you more crap because it's your point of attraction.

How many stories have you heard from people who have managed to turn their whole lives around that start with something like, "I just couldn't stand looking at my surroundings any longer"?

They believed there was something better out there for them without having to know exactly what it might be, and they decided to focus on that great unknown rather than the harsh reality they were experiencing.

They had to set aside their fear of change, their fear of the unknown, and what might be the biggest fear of them all, their fear of what other people might think. That, not coincidentally, brings us back to the title of this chapter, which is "The Root of All Fears."

The fears we have when we're incarnated in this time period on earth are many and varied, but in terms of spiritual advancement, the big kahuna has got to be the fear of being alone. From that single fear, many others are derived: the fear of being different, the fear of not conforming to societal norms, the fear of not fitting in, and the fear of not being connected.

We could examine each of these fears separately, but since they are all so closely related, let's treat them as one universal fear of being alone.

From early childhood, actually more like from birth, we are told in hundreds of ways that we must conform.

Boys wear blue, and girls wear pink. Boys play with cars and trucks, and girls play with dolls. Boys play football, and girls are cheerleaders. Our parents program us to be like all the other kids because—just like our subconscious—they are trying to protect us from being bullied or teased because we are different from "normal kids."

As we get older, especially in middle and high school, we have an absolute terror of not fitting in or being different. We have to wear the same jeans and sneakers as everyone else, and we have to carry the same backpack or we won't fit in and be one of the "cool kids."

When we get to college, there is more leeway, but there is still a persistent fear of not making and having friends. As you get older, you have a fear of not finding your soul mate and having a home and family just like everybody else.

Collectively, most of the subconscious fears you have through all of your life can be traced back to one basic thing: the fear of being alone and disconnected. So, what is the origin of the root of all fears? Where does it come from?

It starts the minute we're born. When the umbilical cord is cut, for the first time in our earth lives, we have a feeling of being completely disconnected and on our own. So, a lot of that crying from newborn babies is them expressing that very unnatural feeling.

When we're at home on the other side—living our real lives—we are always connected to each other, to the unconditional love coming from source, and to the entire universe.

When we arrive here to live another earth life, we have the same sort of amnesia imposed on us about how great it is at home on the other side as we have at home when we're planning our next incarnation.

As a result, when we're planning our earth lives, we have no problem believing that not being connected to everybody and everything is no big deal. Then we get here, and it turns out it's a huge deal.

That constant yearning and searching for a way to feel connected again leads us to be close to our families, make close friends, and on a bigger stage, join clubs, churches, and political parties—anything we can think of to be a part of something larger than ourselves.

In the age of the internet, we can be connected to any number of people around the world at any given time. It's ironic that in an effort to be connected, people will sit alone in a room staring at a computer screen or never look up from their phones when there are actual humans around them.

It seems as if, on the inside, we have a wisp of that memory of what it's like to be connected to the entire universe, so it's a no-brainer to desire the largest network of connections possible. That's what leads people to try to get the greatest number of Facebook friends or Twitter followers. It provides a pale imitation of what it's like on the other side to be at one with the universe.

This cascade of fear, starting with a fear of being different and a fear of what other people think, leads us to believe in the greatest fear: the fear of being alone and disconnected. You might be thinking that it's hopeless. How can anyone possibly cope with and overcome all that negativity?

Fortunately, this big, ugly bundle of fear has one common element that enables us to deal with it. That one thread that we can pull to start unraveling the whole mess is that all the fear and negativity may come from inside us, but it's a reaction to things that are outside of us, and we are able to control our feelings from within.

If you think of yourself as a cell phone charger, then you know you're always looking for a place to plug yourself in so you can charge the phone. All of those plugs are outside of yourself, scattered around our homes, workplaces, and airports.

We know our subconscious is always connected to source, which can provide us with limitless unconditional love from the other side.

Instead of constantly searching for a place to plug in outside of yourself, picture plugging into that internal power source. You don't have to look around for a place to recharge. You already have a source of unending energy inside of you, and it's always available.

Once I came to terms with my subconscious and figured out it was not the enemy keeping me from what I wanted, I realized that it only reflected the negativity I was constantly looking at here on the earth plane.

When I started to focus on the positive, so did my subconscious. Knowing that it is always connected to source, which is only positive at all times, told me that I could recharge anywhere and anytime by plugging into that energy inside myself.

We can only change ourselves from the inside out—not from the outside in. All of our connections to our real lives on the other side reside within us because that is where our subconscious exists.

If we can allow and believe the connection is there, it makes it easier to feel its presence. As always with the law of attraction, if you believe it before you see it, it can only lead to stronger belief and more seeing of the results of that belief.

Jasper has decided to put in an appearance dressed as a medieval knight. He's carrying a lance and stabbing what looks like a large lizard. Now he's offended. He says it's a dragon and that he is Saint George.

Just for clarification, in case you're not a history nerd like me, Saint George is the patron saint of England, and in the Middle Ages, the dragon represented the devil. So even if you still believe there is such a thing as the devil, now you know he was killed by Saint George in the twelfth century, so that's another fear you can put to rest.

Jasper, always unconcerned with historical accuracy but never one to miss a chance to play dress up, says the dragon represents that biggest of fears, being alone and disconnected, and that we can all be our own knights in shining armor. We can kill it once and for all by using the lance of courage and knowledge, and then we will be free from fear, so there.

After that little dramatic interlude, let's sum up what we've learned so we'll have the courage to change and advance in our spiritual journeys.

The root of all fear is the fear of being alone. No one wants to be out there on that cutting edge, forging new trails and paving the way, but somebody has to, so why not you?

Once you realize that all the power you need to actually do that is residing in you all the time, you can easily tap into it by believing what you want and the way you want to get there. It's easier to kill that fear of being alone, which is a positive thing.

Even if moving forward means leaving some of your current friends and family members behind, your new positive vibrations and energy will attract new people to you. Just like in the movies—if you build it, they will come.

When you have those feelings of aloneness at certain times, you can fight them by acknowledging and feeling your connections to the other side through your subconscious, your guides, and anybody else over there who might be taking an interest in how your current earth life is progressing.

And never forget that your connection to source is always present, unbreakable, and able to supply you with unending unconditional love.

12

Lions and Tigers and Bears and Butterflies and Grasshoppers, Oh My

I have mentioned several times in my writings that Jasper, aka Mr. Showbiz, has told me that the other side loves to use movies, TV shows, theater, and even video games to teach us lessons of a spiritual nature.

By using entertainment and popular culture references, they reveal fundamental truths about the way the universe works that we might not be able to grasp if they were presented like a more conventional classroom lecture. They also hope that sending the messages in as many different ways as possible will help us finally be able to "get it."

It's difficult to list all the spiritual information and inspiration in Jasper's all-time favorite "movie with a message." Let me try to point out some of the biggest messages in *The Wizard of Oz* and how they apply to our spiritual journeys.

The beginning of the movie was shot in what is known as black and white, but in reality, it is different variations of gray. And contrary to the titles of recent books and movies, there are way more than fifty shades of gray in the universe.

The message here is that when we incarnate as humans, we want everything to be black or white, good or bad, naughty or nice. It makes it easier to understand people and scenarios if we can put them in to a good or bad category, and it aids us greatly when we start judging everyone around us, a favorite human way to pass the time.

There is very little in the universe that is black or white. That person or scenario you thought was bad or evil probably turned out to be providing you with one of the best learning opportunities you have ever encountered.

I know I keep using my mother and the way she treated me during my childhood as an example, but she doesn't mind now that she has transitioned, so I'll bring her up again. From the way she chose to parent me, I learned, first and foremost, what kind of father not to be with my own daughter. I also learned patience and tolerance, which became very important to me later in life.

If everything around you is "good" and all your relationships are non-confrontational, you are actually making very little forward progress in your spiritual journey. Without seeing, experiencing, and then coming to know what you don't want, there is no impetus to move forward toward what you do want.

You're not seeing the contrast between "good" and "bad" that will give you the push you need to move toward what you consider to be good.

Meanwhile, back in Kansas, after Dorothy's house gets sucked up by a tornado and deposited on top of the Wicked Witch, the movie changes to glorious color. That vibrancy had rarely been seen in a movie before that time, and it is still obvious to anyone watching nearly eighty years later.

At this point, when the colors are at their most strong and vibrant, they can be related to the seven colors of the body chakras, which are our corporeal energy centers.

Dorothy's ruby red slippers are the color of the root chakra, which is associated with passion and danger. What an accurate way to describe the journey she is about to undertake down the yellow brick road; she is following her desires down a path filled with danger.

Yellow, as in the brick road, is the color of the solar plexus chakra, where our courage and strength reside, both of which Dorothy will need in abundance as she sets off to see the Wizard.

Her destination, of course, is the Emerald City, which is green, the color of the heart chakra, representing the earth and nature. She's heading there as a means of finding her way home, literally back to earth.

I'm not any kind of expert on chakras and their meanings, so please do some research on your own if you want to have more insight into how they were used in this movie to send a spiritual message.

My interests lie more in Dorothy's journey, the characters she meets along the way, and how the story relates to our spiritual journey.

The first character she meets in Oz is Glinda the Good Witch, who floats in wearing her impressive crown, waving her magic wand and enclosed in a bubble. I could so see Jasper doing the same thing if given half a chance. Glinda is a perfect stranger, but Dorothy accepts her explanation of what's going on and what she must do to reach her goal of going home.

Come to think of it, that sounds a lot like the relationship I have with Jasper. He sort of just dropped into my life as a stranger and started telling me things I needed to do to help me on my spiritual journey.

It only took a short time for me to accept that he was real, and, in spite of his antics, willing to help me get to my goals. He even helped me to figure out what my goals were by telling me I needed to start writing books.

So, let's say Glinda acts as Dorothy's soul guide in the movie. She gives Dorothy the tools she will need on her journey—the ruby red slippers—and points her in the right direction on the yellow brick road. Dorothy, exhibiting trust in the guidance Glinda has given her, proceeds off toward the Emerald City.

As we know, along the way she meets a scarecrow who thinks he doesn't have a brain, a tin man who thinks he doesn't have a heart, and a lion who thinks he doesn't have courage. The three of them, along with Dorothy, are convinced that the things they want most are "out there" and can be given to them by a magical being known as the Wizard of Oz.

As they move along the yellow brick road, the four friends encounter dangers, both real and imagined, with most of them coming from the Wicked Witch and her flying monkeys. And who among us hasn't had those characters in their lives at home or at work? In the movie, they represent all the fears we talked about in the last chapter.

The important thing we learn from equating the witch and her minions to our fears is that, in the end, no matter how scary they may seem, they can be quickly erased by something as simple as a bucket of water. It can be just as easy to get rid of our own personal fears if we decide to make that happen.

The ultimate message and moral of the story, as you already know if you've seen the movie (if you haven't, stop reading right now and go download it), is that we all possess the knowledge, heart, and courage we need to live out our incarnations if we can just look inside ourselves and believe that those things are already there. It's not necessary to go in search of some magical being that will grant us everything we think we are missing to make us happy.

We also possess our own pair of ruby slippers that can take us wherever we want to go in the form of our connection to our soul guides—if we believe that they are there and willing to help us.

The key to getting our slippers and guides to work for us is contained in one word in that last sentence: *believe*. We have to believe that, before we incarnated for this life, we laid out a yellow brick road that would lead us to whatever learning goal we had set for ourselves and that we have guides in place who will do their best to keep us following that particular path.

Once we have no doubt that our guides are there to help us, our next challenge is to trust and allow them to do just that.

I'm sure we've all seen articles on the internet like, "Twenty-five things flight attendants wish you would stop doing," or "Ten things restaurant servers want you to know." They all involve information that people who work with the public would like to tell you—but would probably be fired for if they did.

There isn't much chance that you're going to fire your soul guide. Jasper is laughing hysterically at the very thought of it. Nevertheless, there are a few things they would like to tell us that we may not want to hear.

First and foremost, when you've done all the spiritual work you need to do to get to the place where you can formulate a goal and then ask your guides to keep you on the path that will get you there, don't keep asking. They heard you the first time, they know your life plan, and they have already placed what you want at the end of the yellow brick road.

Stop repeating yourself. To them, you sound like a toddler saying, "Mom, Mom, Mom, Mommy, Mom, Mommy, Mom," trying to get its mother's attention. It drives them crazy, and if you have a guide like mine who's already halfway there, it can cause a lot of turmoil.

Secondly, remember our new mantra: I believe then I see. Just because what we asked for doesn't show up tomorrow doesn't mean they forgot what we asked for. They aren't Amazon Prime with next-day delivery. They have your request and have diligently fulfilled it. Now it's up to us to do our part, which is to stop looking at the empty place where what we want is supposed to be.

According to the law of attraction, which is what we're trying to learn to use here, if all we can focus on is that what we want isn't here, it will never be here because that is all we are thinking about.

So, what is our part and how do we best play it?

Our job, after we put in the order for what we want, is to work on changing our emotions about that very thing. We have to get to a place of feeling amazing about what is coming before it gets here.

In other words, we have to get ready to get ready. No matter how long it takes, change can't come until we're emotionally ready to receive it.

Let's think back to when we were six or seven years old on the week before Christmas. Remember the barely contained excitement? How the world was filled with Christmas decorations, parties, and special food? How there was a Christmas special on TV every night? Try to recapture that feeling of excitement and the feeling of trust and allowing that came with it.

We all knew—without a shadow of a doubt—that Santa was going to come to our house and bring us toys after we went to sleep on December 24. We didn't know how it happened, but we knew for sure that when we woke up on Christmas morning, there would be presents under the tree for us. By believing they would come, and not caring how, we made those presents appear.

Of course, we all know that our parents made the presents appear, but our guides are like our parents in this instance. They know when we absolutely believe without questioning that what we want will be there. That's what makes it all happen.

Gather up all those childhood feelings and apply them to whatever you have asked the guides to help you attain. Feel that innocent excitement and relearn the feeling of knowing that it will happen just because you believe that it will. Our part in this is adjusting our emotions so that we not only allow and believe it will happen—we expect it to.

Now, because we're trapped here in these human bodies and have only our puny human minds available to us, the guides will give us as much help as they can. They'll leave a trail of bread crumbs we can follow back to our yellow brick road if we wander off the path, as we tend to do.

I asked, "Isn't knowing there are lions, tigers, and bears, oh my, lurking in the forest all along the way enough to keep us on our intended path?"

Jasper said, "Of course not." When we are incarnated here, we fall in love with fear, and what better way to feel that negative emotion than to wander off into the deep, dark jungle unarmed and looking for man-eating beasts?

If we don't see any fierce animals, at least we can hold onto the feelings of fear we wanted, and if we do get attacked by them, we can then claim *victimhood*, which is another negative emotion that we value almost as much as fear.

Are you starting to understand why Jasper, from a place of unconditional love, thinks we're all stupid? Why do we want to not only have fear, anger, and guilt in our lives, but once we have those feelings, cling to them like a drowning man clings to a life preserver?

I think the answer is because they are easy to feel. We have an automatic reaction to fear built into our human bodies; the fight-or-flight response causes a release of certain chemicals into our bloodstream that gives us a certain amount of excitement. It temporarily heightens our senses and makes us feel a little superhuman, if only briefly.

All we have to do to achieve that feeling is be afraid of things in our current life scenarios. It's a perfect explanation for the success of certain cable news outlets that use keeping people in a constant state of fear as their stock in trade.

Anger usually comes along with fear. It's another of the "big three" negative emotions, humans love it almost as much as fear. However, anger doesn't cause any changes in your body chemistry that could be described as good. Quite the opposite.

It can lead to high blood pressure, heart attacks, and strokes, but that doesn't stop people from being angry about anything and everything twenty-four seven.

I guess they feel that if they are angry long enough, then everyone in the world will see that they are absolutely right about everything and change their minds and positions immediately. If this describes your current emotional state, how's that working for you?

Just for the sake of completeness, the third negative emotion in the trilogy is *guilt*. There seems to be a lot less guilt going around currently. I think it's because people get stuck in the anger stage and are absolutely convinced they are right about everything. Why should they feel guilty about hurting anyone else? They deserved what they got, right?

I'm not minimizing the effects of guilt because it can be just as damaging to spiritual growth as fear and anger. Guilt just doesn't have the same physiological effects as the other two.

I'm taking the time to revisit the three ugly stepsisters—fear, anger, and guilt—because when one or all of them are the focus of your daily life, it makes it almost impossible for your soul guides to get through to you and help you deal with and move past those negative emotions.

Your guides dwell in unconditional love, and you have to go to that place for them to communicate fully with you.

If you have fear, anger, and guilt as the major components of your current life scenario, you can't have the unconditional self-love necessary to be able to meet your guides on a level where they can help you.

This is the part where the work comes in. You, and only you, can do the work necessary to clean up all the crap that is holding you back from raising your vibrational energy enough to at least meet your guides halfway.

I've always been a practical, let's-roll-up-our-sleeves-and-get-the-job-done-then-we-can-goof-off kind of guy. If dream catchers and drum circles are working for you and you feel they raise your spiritual vibration and put you in closer touch with the universe, then that's great.

I, however, and I think a lot of people like me, need to know the nuts and bolts of how something works before I can fully understand it.

What it boils down to are two words that I just used: *crap* and *work*. I'm not going to go into great detail about the processes you can use to change your way of thinking. That's an entire book by itself, and I covered much of how I worked through it in my book *Clearing the Track*. A lot of how to do that will also be a large part of my next book. For now, just know that it doesn't happen easily or overnight.

The important thing is that, from earliest childhood, thanks to the constant fear, anger, and guilt we're exposed to on this planet, we start building up large stores of emotional crap, or baggage, if you prefer. The easiest way to deal with it is not to deal with it at all, and just put it all in big steamer trunks and drag it along behind us as we go through life.

If we choose to do that, and then get serious about moving forward in our spiritual journeys, we have to do a lot of very hard work.

We have to take all the time necessary, and it can be a lot, to go through all those trunks, figure out exactly what's in there that is causing us to hold on to our negative emotions, and then deal with it by doing a lot of forgiveness, both of self and others.

If you need help and direction on how to get started doing that, I can heartily recommend my good friend Barb Ruhl's "Power of Self" program available at BarbRuhlHealing.com. It's a weekly lesson and meditation on all aspects of the self that takes a year to complete, which is a small amount of time to invest in improving your life.

If you find yourself in a place where you don't know which direction to take, and you feel that you don't have any connection to your guides, don't despair. Even if you don't feel the presence of your guides, they are always there and are trying to help you.

There will be times when even the most connected person will sort of backslide in regard to their vibrational energy and go to where they have self-doubt or maybe even stop liking themselves. I know I personally have been in a place where I developed a fear of something not happening while at the same time having a fear that it would happen. How screwed up is that?

I really needed to take time to unravel that emotional knot, and Jasper was a big help for a change by assisting me in thinking through why I felt the way I did. He was able to help me through the mess I had put myself in because I never went into a self-doubt or self-hate mode. I was just fearful and confused for a brief time.

In spite of your guides loving you unconditionally always and forever, there may be times when they are not able to communicate fully with you.

Jasper calls these periods "reverse time-outs." When I get out of control, instead of sending me to a corner to think about how I'm behaving, he sends himself to a corner until I'm done with whatever little drama I think I have to put myself through. After I get back to a place of loving myself, he can come back and talk to me again.

There is a difference between being confused or troubled about a decision or scenario and not unconditionally loving yourself.

Your guides can't help you with a problem if that problem is causing you to dislike or doubt yourself.

Once you get to that place of complete self-acceptance, you have to fight like hell to stay there because it's the only way to stay connected at all times to your guides.

When we start to go astray, to help us get back on track—back on our yellow brick roads, so to speak—the other side will send us little clarifications, which they call "butterflies."

Messages in the form of these spiritual butterflies are directional signs and little pieces of encouragement sent by your guides to get you to feel the emotions of having what you are wanting and waiting for.

In a session with Barb, when we first learning about the butterflies, I thought, *Here we go—butterflies and unicorns. Sunshine, lollipops, and rainbows. More New Agey BS.* But after I got a more thorough explanation from the guides, I realized it's not like that.

Butterflies are used as a metaphor because they're pretty, they attract attention, and they fly free. People enjoy looking at them. Because of their beauty, we are naturally drawn to looking at them. By packaging the clarifications your guides are sending as something that makes you feel good just to look at, it's easier for them to get you to stop looking at whatever negativity you are focused on.

So, what are the butterflies? They are anything that makes you feel a positive emotion, ranging from simple joy to absolute bliss, even if only for a fleeting moment.

It may be seeing a rainbow or hearing a child's laughter. It may be finding that twenty-dollar bill in the pocket of a coat you haven't worn in a while when you need a little extra cash. It may be seeing an old picture that brings back a good memory or getting a message from a friend you haven't heard from in some time.

One of the ways I have noticed that the other side is trying to reach out is that a song will come on the radio that you seldom hear, and it brings back a good memory, or the lyrics seem to fit perfectly with whatever you're going through.

The guides say they can send us a hundred or more butterflies per day, but Jasper says most of us ignore 99 percent of them—or we don't recognize that they are there to give us a little bit of joy. We need to remember that there are no such things as coincidences and pay more attention to these small encouragements that our guides are sending our way.

Now, because we are human and are doing the best we can with our puny human minds, we occasionally will get distracted by a grasshopper, or a negative thought, because they can be interesting to look at and watch. They'll draw us off the path and into the tall weeds at the side of the road.

That's okay for a while because we may be looking at some emotion that we still need to work on that may be on the negative side. Always remember, though, that when you're looking down at the grasshopper and stumbling around in the weeds, you're off the path and not moving forward.

The way to resume making progress is to start looking up and searching for those butterflies again. You do that by choosing to feel good—even for a brief period of time. The bottom line is that it's about the feeling more than the path.

If we believe we can only feel good if we are getting what we want, then we are making our happiness conditional on that happening. Being unconditional means we're deciding to feel good no matter what happens, and only by doing that can we manifest what we really want.

More than twenty years ago, Lorrie Morgan had a big country hit called "Except for Monday." The lyrics were about getting over a broken heart: "Except for Monday, which was never good anyway. Tuesday, I get a little sideways. Wednesday, I feel better just for spite."

That's the attitude we all need to have when we're dealing with our crap and trying to move away from whatever we're carrying in our emotional baggage. Say to yourself, "I'm going to feel better just for spite, if nothing else."

You have to continuously work at wearing down your resistance to thinking and believing you can't change your situation just by deciding you want to. You absolutely can, and your guides will be thrilled to help you do it.

It's so easy for us to get sidetracked by the scenarios playing out in our lives and all around us that we can forget the butterflies are even there. Fortunately, our guides never forget that even though we may be chasing grasshoppers and filling jars with them, our real desire is to have a jar full of butterflies, and they will do everything they can to help us refocus and remember.

What happens if you're dense, like Jasper says I am, and don't see the butterflies your guides are sending your way? Well, the J-man says people like us (I know I'm not the only one), can imagine we have a butterfly stamp and use it to create butterflies out of any situation.

Just as an example, let's say you are not completely enjoying your current job and are having difficulty maintaining the level of happiness throughout your workday that you would like.

Set a goal of being happy until your morning break, and if you make it, give yourself a butterfly stamp on the back of your hand. Then try to be happy until lunch. If you make it, give yourself another stamp. If your boss or a coworker should happen to give you a compliment, stamp. Got through the afternoon without any suicidal thoughts? Stamp. Made it home without having a case of road rage? Stamp.

You don't have to wait for the other side to send you a butterfly you may or may not see, even though it's great when they do and you can recognize them. Make your own and tailor them to any life scenario you are having problems dealing with.

This journey you're on is all about you and your self-improvement. It takes a lot of work, but there's no reason the work can't be fun at least part of the time. And always remember that being selfish is not always a bad thing—and taking care of yourself emotionally and spiritually is never bad.

I'm aware that this book contains a lot of information, and some of it may seem fantastic and unbelievable to many readers. I have found in my dealings with all the teachers on the other side that if I'm not getting something the way they are presenting it, they will try another way until I get at least a minimum of understanding.

Hence all of Jasper's costume changes and playing out excerpts from old TV shows and movies. He keeps throwing things at my puny human mind until something sticks.

I've attempted to do the same thing here. If something I've written doesn't make sense to you, keep reading because, hopefully, something will later on.

The one overriding thing I hope everyone takes away from this book is a shift in the way we think about our spiritual journeys and the universe at large. As humans, we have no trouble at all believing we can and will have failures in our lives. Why can't we believe just as strongly that we can and will have great success?

Our beliefs are just thoughts we keep thinking. Instead of dwelling only on the negative, keep thinking about all the positives—and you will come to believe them.

I send you nothing but love and light as we all continue on our own spiritual journeys, and I hope all the information I have shared has been of some help.

13

Preview of Guidespeak

Over the course of the past few years, it's become apparent to me that almost no part of our spiritual journeys is as important as allowing, believing, and trusting in the existence of our soul guides. However, accomplishing that can be no small feat for many people.

If you aren't in a place of self-awareness that holds as truth the unconditional love of self, it can be very difficult to accept that there are beings in the universe who love you unconditionally and whose only purpose is to help you.

Even after you get to that place of self-acceptance, the next step is learning to contact and have conversations with your guides. Once we know we can be in constant contact with them, and they are able to point us in the direction we want to go in our current incarnation, the sky is no longer the limit.

Because the guides are living on the other side, they are immersed in nothing but positive energy and the unconditional love that binds the whole universe together.

The whole universe, that is, except for one tiny little exception: planet earth. This small planet we've all chosen to incarnate on is the only one, as far as I know, where negativity is the norm. Just as unconditional love and positivity are taken for granted in the universe at large, the earth exists as a showcase for negativity of every type and description.

It sounds like an extremely bad thing, but it serves a very important purpose. It allows those souls that are strong enough and have a burning desire to incarnate here as many times as they want to experience that negativity. Only by doing that can they know it up close and personal, so to speak.

By living in an atmosphere of nearly total negativity, and fighting not to become part of it, we learn coping skills that follow us through all of our lives and make us spiritually stronger as a result.

Soul guides have always been part of the equation when planning an earth life, but as the atmosphere of this dimension has become increasingly negative, their roles as the ones who can provide much-needed direction and encouragement has become exponentially more important.

Whether you call them guides, guardian angels, or intuition—or think of them as a little voice in the back of your mind—living out a successful incarnation without them would be next to impossible.

Of course, as Jasper loves to remind us, because we only have access to about 10 percent of our intellect when we come here, many of us stupidly blunder around going from bad life scenario to worse life scenario, thinking we can handle things all on our own. That was the case for me for the largest part of my life. In fact, after I got reacquainted with my guides, they thought it was hilarious that I had chosen to live the first part of my life with only minimal input from them.

After regaining direct access to them, I didn't think it was funny at all that I had kept them on the sidelines, but that was all my doing and planning. I learned to cope with a lot of negativity while they were just watching events unfold. Everything happens for a reason.

So due to the ever-increasing need for people incarnated on earth to have access to and help from their soul guides, this book is going to delve more deeply into the who, what, when, where, and why of them, and hopefully bring about a better understanding of how to hear them more clearly—and how they can help us once we do.

Along the way, we're going to be looking in more depth at those three ugly stepsisters—anger, fear, and guilt—and how they can block communication with our guides.

When we choose, and it is a choice, to hold on to anger, fear, and guilt for long periods of time without trying to get to the bottom of why we're doing that, and more importantly, trying to deal with those negative emotions to get rid of them, we can block nearly all communication from our guides. They simply can't reach us when we are totally focused on negativity, especially when it applies to how we feel about ourselves.

Our guides know that we are totally amazing beings for even deciding to come here in the first place, but they have no way to reach us if we are in a constant state of self-doubt or self-loathing. It's like we only speak and understand Mandarin Chinese, and they only speak and understand Greek. There may be some gesturing and pantomime, but there is no real communication.

My goal, along with all the guides on the other side, is to provide enough information in this book to get everyone in direct contact with their soul guides on a daily basis—just as I am with mine.

Hopefully, yours will be a little more compassionate and understanding than mine. Since they act the way you instructed them to while you were doing the planning for this life, you can't complain about their personalities. You brought whatever form they come in on yourself.

Jasper has a whole new wardrobe lined up, and since this book is about him and his kind, he can't wait to take center stage. So, as they say, let the adventure begin.